"Tiny Time Big Re
fresh air in the wor
Dale Beaumont, Founder & CEO of Business Blueprint & Bizversity

TINY TIME
BIG RESULTS

4 Principles to Run
Your Profitable
20-Hour Week Business

YASMIN VORAJEE

Published by Stardust Publishing House

Print ISBN: 978-1-9164761-0-3

eBook ISBN: 978-1-9164761-1-0

Front Cover Design: eBook Designs

Book Interior: eBook Designs

For print or media interviews, please contact support@yasminvorajee.com

Visit the website: www.yasminvorajee.com

To get the most out of this book and the Tiny Time community, join the **Tiny Time Book Club** and get instant access to your accompanying workbook and resources. Join here www.yasminvorajee.com/jointtbookclub

For Colm, Fionn, Zayna and Daire

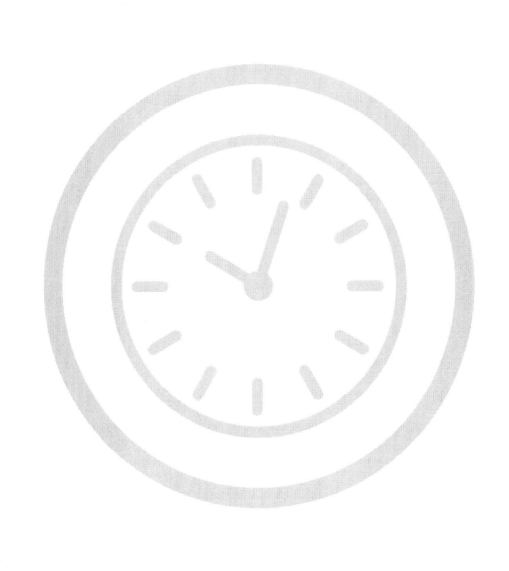

PRAISE FOR TINY TIME BIG RESULTS: THE BOOK!

"Tiny Time Big Results is a breath of fresh air in the world of business books, because it shows us once and for all there is another way to build a great business. One where you don't have to burn the midnight oil and sacrifice your family, your health or your soul. Well done Yasmin!
Dale Beaumont - Founder & CEO of Business Blueprint & Bizversity, www.businessblueprint.com

"A practical, warm and above all doable approach to making a business work on your terms. Yasmin walks her talk, and sets out a clear set of principles for valuing your time and creating a valuable business too."
Alison Jones, Publisher and Host of The Extraordinary Business Book Club

'Tiny Time, Big Results' is the voice, heart & knowledge I need right now. I love how you feel your hand is held throughout the book ensuring your business fits into your values, goals, family and life through Yasmin's step by step process. Nothing is left unturned in a really gentle way.

It's much needed in today's society to empower those who want to live a balanced & successful lifestyle as an entrepreneur. It's my new best friend! It really helped me address the internal chatter I had going on that I thought I was alone in and not only made me feel normal but actually helped me resolve those niggly things I hadn't noticed were really holding me back.

The enthusiasm, simplified problem solving and solutions offered are so effective. Thank you!
**Karen Dwyer, Speaker, Coach, Trainer,
www.karendwyer.global**

"Whether you're only starting out on your entrepreneurial journey or are further along in your business, Yasmin's clear no-nonsense approach in this book will help you cut through the sense of overwhelm and overload that comes with running your own business whilst juggling other responsibilities. Written in an accessible and easy to digest way, peppered with real world examples, it will save you so much time trying to figure out everything on your own."
**Miriam Reilly, Yoga Nidra Teacher, Blogger,
Self-love Coach www.miriamreilly.com**

"I loved this book because it shows you exactly how to generate results, using just a small amount of your time. I particularly enjoyed the simplicity of the explanations and methodology. It is easy to read and put into practice, giving me the confidence to start.

I would recommend this book as Yasmin's own journey is intertwined throughout, offering an honest insight revealing how to replicate her processes. It is refreshing that Yasmin is practicing what she preaches. I always felt I never had time, but since reading this book, I have used my "tiny time" to start my journey to create a new business I have been sitting on for a year. A "must have" for anyone who thinks they don't have time."
Dan Mangion, www.staypositive.com.au

"This book sets out that there is a way to business success without the need to work constantly and at the expense of other important aspects of life. With her clear plans for getting your message right, having confident conversations with potential clients, and adopting the right mindset, Yasmin has created a fantastic guide to how you can thrive in your business. You will feel like you have plenty of time in the week to focus on the success you desire!"
Meg Lyons, Coach, www.meglyons.com

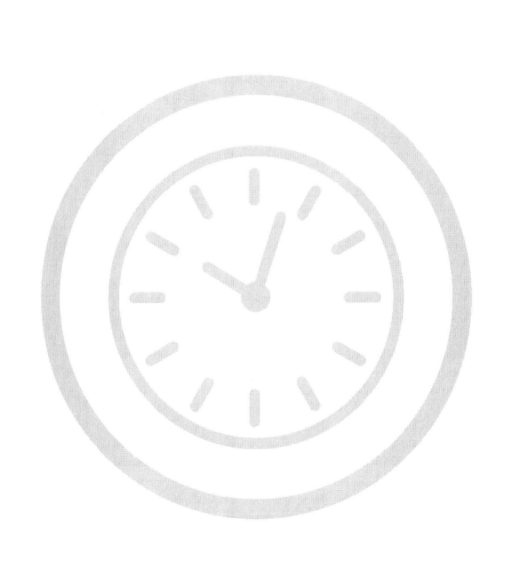

CONTENTS

SECTION 1:
SET THE SCENE

*"An investment in knowledge
pays the best interest."*

— Benjamin Franklin

CHAPTER 1: INTRODUCTION

The day I was paid £3,000 for a 30-minute talk was the day my life changed forever. I was new in business and had been asked to share my perspective on coaching in the workplace to the annual conference of an accountancy firm.

I was able to put together the speech quickly as I'd been coaching and teaching coaching skills to managers in the workplace for seven years at that point. I travelled to the UK from Ireland and delivered my half-hour presentation.

And I was paid £3,000 for something I could and would have easily done for free. I was stunned at the effortlessness of creating value from what I knew and turning it into money in the bank.

This is what I want for you.

This book is about how to package and position your experience, expertise and knowledge into a profitable and productive business in 20 hours a week or less. You might have a family, you might not, you might be planning to have one in the future or you might just want a business that works in the time you choose to dedicate to it. This book and this journey is about designing your business so it fits into your life. A business that works for you, not you working for it.

You might not think it's possible to run a business in 20 hours a week. The narrative around business glorifies long work hours and sacrificing everything else for the greater good.

I have a different view...

The truth is we live in an age of uncertainty. When my son was 15 months old, I lost my corporate job of 12 years, the job that had supported me and my family. My husband and I wanted to have more children and I didn't want to be a commuter mum; seeing my children in the morning, sending them to childcare and school, picking them up in the evening for a couple of precious hours, then starting the routine all over again the next day. I wanted to be there for my children and I also wanted to fulfil my own ambitions. I couldn't do that in the workplace. Not in the workplace as I knew it anyway.

I don't believe modern working life is compatible with a healthy family life. We are pulled in too many directions and it's exhausting. I see it with friends and colleagues all the time. And modern working life is especially incompatible with women fulfilling their potential. How can it be when your prospects and income opportunities fall off a cliff simply because you choose to start a family?

I see another way...

In the 21st century, here in the West, nobody has a job for life nor do we want one. When I was growing up, my siblings and I were taught to get a good education, then a good job and work till retirement. We are not working to this outdated life view anymore. Times have changed considerably. We are living longer, job instability has increased and technology has revolutionised how we live and work.

Yet we stay in unfulfilling jobs because we need the money; we have bellies to feed and mortgages to pay. We continue to work until retirement and pay into a pension, even though the idea that we pay into a pot of money that will sustain us for 20 to 30 years after we finish working is *lunacy* when life expectancy has increased, inflation reduces the value of your money and the only certainty you have is a reduced standard of living as that pot dwindles. Meanwhile, we hope we'll have time do all the things we've always wanted to do.

And that might be fine for most people but I know you want more. More freedom, more flexibility and more time with your loved ones. You want to do work that fills your purse and your soul. I believe you can do this on your own terms.

Over the last 15 to 20 years, we have seen a huge growth in people starting their own businesses, selling their skills and knowledge. Technological advances makes this easier than ever before and the advent of social media means we can start to trade almost immediately. This has been especially revolutionary for the women who attempt to navigate the minefield that is raising a family! It's revolutionary for those who care for their elderly parents and loved ones and revolutionary for those who seek a lifestyle on their terms.

There are real opportunities for people like you and me, people with skills, gifts and talents to turn them into healthy incomes and live the lives of our dreams. I'm not talking about 'a little extra pocket money', which is sometimes used to describe the money women make. I'm talking about real wealth. Real wealth created from selling what you know.

As author and coach Michael Neill once said, 'Financial security is not the amount of money you have in the bank; it's knowing you can make money when you need it'. There is something truly wonderful about making money and knowing you have created that value. Herein lies true freedom.

This is my dream for you.

"There are real opportunities for people like you and me, people with skills, gifts and talents to turn them into healthy incomes and live the lives of our dreams."

CHAPTER 2: THIS BOOK IS FOR YOU IF...

You want to run and grow a profitable and fulfilling business based on your expertise, experience, knowledge and passions in 20 hours a week or less.

But you're not there yet...

You might lie in bed at night worrying where the next client will come from. Or you know you need to market your business and get really good at sales, but you hate the thought of hustling. Maybe you wonder, *how on earth can I grow the business when I have so little time?*

You've chosen this book because you feel the pressure of 'not having enough time' and want to stop feeling this way. You have big dreams and desires. You want to share your message, earn great money and make a real difference without working long hours. You want freedom and flexibility in how you work so you're not constrained by the rules of others. But sometimes it all feels too big and amorphous. You find it hard to break down the vision into meaningful and specific actions that move you closer to your dreams.

It doesn't matter if you've been in business for a while or you're just starting out. This book will show you how to make money doing what you're good at and love in 20 hours a week or less, so you can enjoy the best of everything life has to offer. Life is an amazing adventure and yet we have trapped ourselves into thinking we're here only to pay the bills instead of following our hearts, making the world a better place just by being in it, serving others, and making life easier and better for so many.

It's my intention to help you have a business that makes your heart and purse sing like when you're in the shower and you don't care who hears!

Ready?

You've chosen this book because you feel the pressure of 'not having enough time' and want to stop feeling this way. You have big dreams and desires. You want to share your message, earn great money and make a real difference without working long hours.

CHAPTER 3: WHAT YOU'LL GET FROM THIS BOOK

It took about three years to write *Tiny Time Big Results* and there is a reason why it took so long. I was still figuring this stuff out. (And I continue to do so!) I submitted a sample of the book to an editor and her questions created a lightbulb moment... I realised what I had written was about two years out of date! I was writing the wrong book.

I wanted the book to be the book I wished I'd had when I first started. Instead, I had written a book that did not truly reflect what I have learned on this journey.

I decided to start again. In one month, I re-wrote the whole book from scratch. Now it's the book I know I would have wanted to read back then.

In *Tiny Time Big Results: 4 Principles to Run Your Profitable 20-Hour Week Business*, I'm going to share with you my approach to making your business work in 20 hours a week or less. I'm not a guru. I don't promise that if you follow my secret formula (there is no secret formula), you'll have a business that spews out money for you all day and all night without you having to do anything. If anyone promises you that, run from them as fast as you can! This work is not easy. If it was, everyone would do it. But it is simple.

What is worthwhile takes effort and attention.

But if you want to turn your expertise, passion and skills into a profitable business, I will show you how (with no hype or BS). It doesn't matter if you've been in business for 10+ years or you're just starting out. I will show you the key steps you need to think about in order to attract clients and cash consistently, and how to leverage the time you have so you can grow the business without sacrificing your time.

You've chosen this book because you feel the pressure of 'not having enough time' and want to stop feeling this way. You have big dreams and desires. You want to share your message, earn great money and make a real difference without working long hours.

I'm not a guru. I don't promise that if you follow my secret formula (there is no secret formula), you'll have a business that spews out money for you all day and all night without you having to do anything. If anyone promises you that, run from them as fast as you can!

CHAPTER 4: WHAT THIS BOOK ISN'T

You know what this book is; now let's look at what it's not! Just because something has worked for one person does not mean it will work for you. That's why this book is not about secret formulas or telling you to replicate something that worked for me.

You shouldn't have to entrust your decision-making to other people to know what's best for you. You can rely on your own wisdom and intuition. You already have an inner business expert, the part of you that knows what steps to take. My job is to help you learn the principles and apply them to your business. So you don't have to rely on others. You can rely on yourself.

It is *your* business after all.

This book is grounded in principles and concepts. As you read the book, ask yourself, how could I make this work in my business? Keep asking yourself this question and think of yourself as a coffee pot... let it percolate. Don't push for the answers. Allow them to come to you. Give them space to rise up from within you. You have amassed experience and knowledge that you can turn into a valuable business. What I want to show you is the process and sequence to do just that. Business is a series of steps in a particular sequence. This book shows you those steps and the sequence so you don't make expensive and time-consuming mistakes, like many others did, like I did.

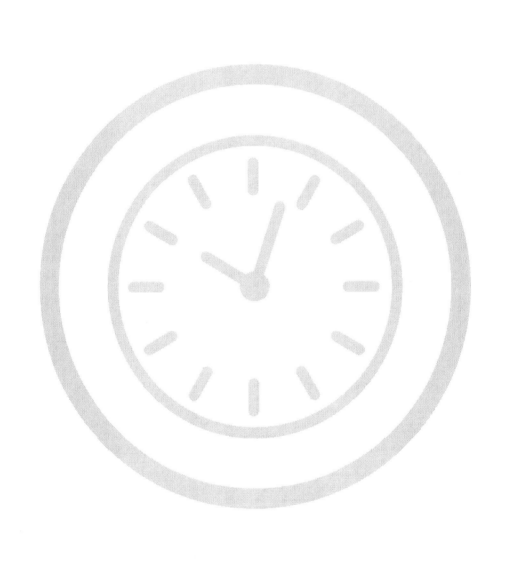

CHAPTER 5: WHO AM I AND HOW DID IT START?

Before we get into 'my story', I want to tell you this is not a rags-to-riches tale. No welfare to millions. No big accident or near-death experience to miraculous recovery. No Road-to-Damascus conversions. Sorry! There were plenty of moments of decision and destiny, but nothing as dramatic as some stories you'll hear.

My story is an ordinary story about an ordinary girl. I have never slept in my car (thankfully) or hit rock bottom (and hope to God I never do). Many people have, I realise, but don't you sometimes feel like having some incredible hero story is a prerequisite for going into business these days? Well, I don't have a story like that. And what's more, I know you don't need one.

I grew up in a three-bedroom terraced house in Preston, Lancashire in the late 1970s. I'm of the generation that played outside all day and only came home when it got dark. I can remember when Google wasn't your source of information — it was the library! I am the youngest of three, our parents are from India, and I was raised in a Muslim family. Like many Indian parents, ours were keen to make sure we got a good education, found good secure jobs and lived good moral lives. Nothing too out-of-the-ordinary there.

I went to school, worked hard (loved English and history, struggled with maths) and did what was expected. But I always had this little rebel inside me, wanting more! I had a desire to do my own thing. After school and college, I went to York University and got a degree in politics and sociology. Alongside my studies, I dabbled in entrepreneurship — multi-level marketing like Amway and NuSkin, and importing Indian clothes (where I never got further than designing the website!)

I grew up seeing women struggle to juggle work and home life. It was portrayed as stressful and hard work. Think *Baby Boom* with Diane Keaton! Deep down, I knew that when I had my own family, I wanted freedom and flexibility so I could be there for my children and not worry about money. But it didn't happen that way.

I left university and went straight into a summer job in a call centre. I graduated on the Thursday; on the Monday, I started work.

And I stayed with the company for 12 years!

Within nine months of starting, I moved from the call centre to my dream job as a training co-ordinator. I remained in that job for just over a year and then decided to move to Ireland to experience another country for a couple of years. (I'm still here!) I continued working my way up the career ladder and became an HR co-ordinator, a training team leader, a training manager, a facilitator and eventually Vice President of Leadership Development. During that time, I became accredited as an Executive and Life Coach, certified as an NLP practitioner, achieved my chartered membership of the CIPD (Chartered Institute of Personnel and Development), married my sweetheart and had our bouncing baby boy! I focused heavily on personal development during that time too, attending courses and events.

Life was good and I knew my job inside out, but I struggled wondering how I'd progress in the corporate jungle and balance my family needs. I was the main earner. My husband looked after our son. Yet I didn't know how to move forward to make my own dream come true... the dream of having my own business. I wanted to believe passionately in what I was doing and I didn't get that fulfilment from corporate.

In the end, the Universe answered my prayers and I was made redundant. This was 2011 when the globe was in a financial meltdown.

Finally... my time had come!

So there I was, January 2012, fresh-faced and excited... And so naïve!

I started working with a coach and she helped me start shaping what I wanted my business to do. (In an ideal world, I would have started my business while still working, but my company's policy didn't allow it... and I couldn't risk my job). *Hint: if you want to start a business, and you already have a job, but no obstacles, start!!*

A month after I began, I miscarried my baby at seven weeks and was devastated. It shook me and I don't know what I did for the next couple of months. Nonetheless, I continued working with my lovely coach and gradually put myself out there... with no clue about what I did, who my service was for or how I served those people.

I focused on what comes easily to me (time management, organisation, planning) and shared that with prospects. I landed my first client through networking. Slowly, the trickle increased to a flow and I continued to refine my message. Months passed. And while I had *some* clients, I was not making great money at all! I watched my little boy get bigger and just kept plugging away at this business thing.

In November that year, I attended an event in Dublin and decided I needed the support of a mentoring group. I signed up for a group program for 12 months and made some brilliant friends. I joined thinking, *Now I'll get sorted*. Uhhhhmmmm....nope!

Problem was I still didn't know what I was doing. I was getting results from my coaching clients (improving their time management, organising their businesses, helping them craft great business plans and building support teams), but I didn't have a compelling hook. I didn't have that special something to entice new clients to work with me or a neat way of explaining what my business was about. And that made explaining and selling what I did so hard!

I also discovered I was pregnant again. Now the pressure was on to have a fully functioning business by the time I had the baby in the middle of 2013.

That didn't happen either!

Yes, this is the tale of all the not-great stuff that happened to me on my journey. If your story is like mine, full of twists and turns and not always lots of progress and certainly no rags-to-riches linear path to 'seven-figure success'... you're in great company!

I was still grappling with my niche, my 'hook', so I decided to switch from working with business owners to working with women in corporate.

I created the Ruby Shoes Revolution. (Think Dorothy and the Wizard of Oz.) My mission? To help emerging women leaders. After all, I was an expert in training and leadership.

I took part in the Global Women and Leadership Summit, alongside Cherie Blair, Marianne Williamson, John Gray and many more amazing speakers. It was fantastic but my heart wasn't in corporate any more, if it ever had been. Plus, getting buying decisions from corporates is a long-winded process. There was no alignment between the corporate audience of that summit and the direction my business needed to go.

I still participated in the monthly mentoring group I'd signed up for, but I was seriously struggling. Money was haphazard. I was getting more and more pregnant. And I was Stressed with a capital 'S'!

I kept wishing, *If only I could get clear on my niche!*

I had my baby girl in July and decided to take some time to enjoy her (best decision ever). Even though financially we weren't doing great, we were still hanging in there. I attempted a launch a few months later and it flopped. At this point, I questioned everything. By the time the new year came round, I knew I had to get this sorted and the choice was stark...

Make it work or get a job.

Now I had two children and definitely did not want to be a commuter mum. We live in rural Ireland and jobs were not aplenty! Nor did I want to go back to an office environment. That wasn't and still isn't the life I imagined for myself. I went to an event in London to see if I could get inspired and motivated. The event was brilliant but I still didn't have a compelling hook! It got to March of 2014 and I was fading fast. A little over two years in and it was not looking good. I was heart-sore. Nothing was working. I had invested so much money, time and effort, and was still no closer.

By chance, I watched a video by a coach I knew. I was intrigued by what she shared and decided I needed her help. I didn't know what I was doing. Doing it alone was not working for me or my bank account. I checked out her coaching packages and made a decision to hire her one-on-one to get her eyes on my business.

Hiring a coach or mentor can be a scary proposition. You have to consider the time investment, the financial investment and the return on investment (which isn't always measured in monetary terms). I made the decision to invest at this stage because it felt like I had nothing to lose. I had tried doing this by myself and it had not worked. I needed someone who was just a few steps ahead of me to show me the way. Not in a 'here's the secret formula' way. (You already know I don't believe there's a special formula!) But in a 'show me how it *could* work for me' way.

Finally, I had the support I needed. My coach helped me see what I couldn't. The work I had done and clients I had worked with weren't in vain. And I *did* have a hook. A compelling one! I was just too close to see it. My coach helped me see the value in my business.

By the end of our first session, **Tiny Time Big Results** was born.

CHAPTER 6: IT'S NEVER BLACK AND WHITE

Tiny Time Big Results was born but that doesn't mean it was plain sailing from then on. That was just the beginning! Then I had to turn this concept into a real business, with paying clients! It took time for me to figure it all out. And I still am! But while I struggled with my niche, carving out my space and what I wanted to be known for, I was still showing up and serving my clients.

You might find yourself getting disheartened that things are not happening as fast as you would like. I get that. I get impatient too. But instead of getting disheartened and stopping your marketing or selling (a sneaky self-sabotage trick), please keep this in mind...

You will not find clarity in your head. You create clarity by doing. You will refine and hone through the simple act of consistently showing up and serving your clients.

Over the last six years of running my own business, I have run several online group programs, facilitated masterminds, created many online courses, sold VIP packages and upgraded my business skills by learning how to write copy, make sales pages, web pages and opt-in pages, set up courses and create a solid

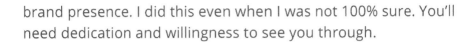
brand presence. I did this even when I was not 100% sure. You'll need dedication and willingness to see you through.

As you can imagine, I have learnt a lot about what to do and also what not to do. This means you don't have to make the same mistakes I made, saving you time, money and tears.

This book is your secret weapon.

You will not find clarity in your head. You create clarity by doing. You will refine and hone through the simple act of consistently showing up and serving your clients.

CHAPTER 7: WHAT IS TINY TIME?

I define tiny time as limited time to put towards your business. You might have four or five hours a day. Maybe just two or three like me. Or you might work a day or two per week. Essentially, tiny time encapsulates the limited pockets of time we have to get things done.

My tiny time is down to me balancing the growth of my business with raising my family. It is a conscious choice and decision to make the business work in a limited time and this is the journey I will be taking you on too.

As I show you how you can make this work for you, there are four key principles we will cover. Tiny Time Big Results is built on the principles of **Purpose, Profit, Productivity and Play**. To make your business work in tiny time, each principle gives you a fresh approach for how to work.

This is not a linear process. You don't move from one principle to the other in a step-by-step fashion. It is a never-ending circle. You will revisit each aspect a number of times and that's how it's meant to be.

The Purpose Principle

This is the why behind everything you do, not just your overall reason for being, but the motivation behind your income goals, what you do, who you serve, the products you sell, the content you create, the hours you work.

The Profit Principle

This is how you make money in your business and the actions you take to make it happen.

The Productive Principle

This how you organise the limited time you have. Work expands to fill the time available for it and business owners are so good at being busy, but I want you to be productive for the right reasons.

The Play Principle

All work and no play is not a recipe for a fulfilling and successful life or business. If you don't make time to enjoy what you're doing, have fun with it and take time away from your work, you will burn out. You can't be who you're meant to be when you're running on empty.

CHAPTER 8: HOW TO USE THIS BOOK

To get the most out of this book, I would encourage you to read from start to finish first, then go back and work through the sections using the accompanying workbook, which you can download when you join the Book Club at www.yasminvorajee.com/jointtbookclub

It's designed so that you can dip in and out of the sections you need. It is both conceptual and practical. This is not about adding a huge amount of work to your day. It's about being smart and savvy about how you use this information, and more importantly, how you apply it.

If you're just starting out, don't be afraid or overwhelmed by what I cover in this book. Think of this book as your companion. Take what you need from it and use the workbook (available when you join the Book Club at www.yasminvorajee.com/jointtbookclub) to guide your journey.

If you don't want to do this alone and you want more support, guidance and implementation, then your next step would be to join the Tiny Time Business School, a program that takes you through the nuts and bolts of how to make the Tiny Time principles work for you, attract clients and cash consistently, and leverage your business so you can grow and scale.

You can find out more about the Tiny Time Business School here: www.yasminvorajee.com/tinytimebusinessschool.

Remember, you do not have to do it all immediately. You take this journey step by step, piece by piece. My mantra is 'tiny steps taken consistently create big leaps'.

Nobody starts off with all the answers. For a long time, I thought everyone else except me had the recipe book or roadmap and that was why they were doing so much better than I was. It felt like I was the only one struggling. Which was not true. It's not true for you now either. The reality is we do the best we can with what we know and what we have. Some people are ahead of us and some are still to learn what you already know. It doesn't matter! It's not a race. It's a journey.

Join the Book Club www.yasminvorajee.com/jointtbookclub/, get your copy of the workbook and follow along at your own pace.

SECTION 2: WHERE IT GOES WRONG

Don't waste a good mistake…
Learn from it!

— **Robert Kiyosaki**

When you have tiny time, knowing what to focus on is key. But knowing what can trip you up is even more powerful. This section outlines the problems that will stop you from making progress in your tiny-time business. So you can see them coming and side-step them neatly!

CHAPTER 9: THE ELEPHANT IN THE ROOM

Before we get going, I want to make something clear from the outset. You will notice as you read this book that the most detailed and meaty principle is the Profit Principle, the money you make in your business. This is deliberate.

It frustrates me when business owners tell me they are not doing it for the money, that money does not motivate them, and that they have a 'higher calling' than something as lowly as money. If you have uttered these words, first of all, no judgement. However, I would also like to invite you to rethink this attitude. If you tell yourself the 'story' that money doesn't matter and then wonder why you're not making any, this is for you.

Money is a form of exchange in our world. It's how we buy goods and services. It's how we fulfil our daily needs like food, water, heating, lighting etc. It is not dirty. It is not 'unspiritual'. It's just currency.

In the olden days, people bartered for goods...

"I'll give you a chicken if you fix my roof."

"I'll look after your children if you cook my meals."

People bartered with all sorts: from the use of their animals or property to their skills or craft. When you put it like that and realise it's an exchange, it sounds crazy to say that money is not important.

If you struggle with asking for money, then just for the purpose of this exercise, pretend you're asking for a chicken. Tell yourself you need 100 chickens so you can exchange them for food and heating. Replace money with chickens and you soon start to see it simply as currency.

"Chickens are not important to me."

But if chickens are the way you buy goods and services, feed and clothe your family, then they are important, because without those 100 chickens, you have no clothes or food. Money is the same. Money is how we get what we need. We all need money to sustain us. Some need more than others and that's dependent on your lifestyle. But when you say money is not important to you, you push it away. You may find you attract people who also say the same thing. And guess what. They have no money either!

This is my reality: I love money. I love money for the choices it creates for me. I love money because I can use it to make life easier for myself and my family. If my son wants to take music lessons, I can pay for them. I can afford my daughter's ballet lessons easily. I can hire a cleaner so I don't have to spend my 'free' time cleaning. We can take lovely holidays. We can enjoy life. I no longer have to worry if my card will be declined as I stand in line waiting to pay for groceries. (I've been there too many times before.) I know what it's like to have €50 in the bank and wonder how we'll pay the mortgage. Too many people are stuck at the sustenance level and it's not pretty.

When you worry constantly about the basics, you have no head or heart space to think about living a fuller life, making a positive difference in the world and enjoying yourself.

You cannot do your best work when you are worried.

The creative energy is lost.

I deliberately emphasise the need to run a *profitable* business because this is how our world works and you need money to live fully and abundantly.

I started my business after redundancy from a 12-year corporate career. My location meant that if I tried getting a similar job, it would be two hours each way every day. I wasn't up for that commute! I also wanted more children. In our modern-day system, family life and working life are not compatible. There's a trade-off: either spend time with your family or make a living. That was not a trade-off I was interested in.

Starting my business when my eldest was 15 months old then having two more children meant I could breastfeed for as long as I wanted. I didn't have to worry about leaving my babies in childcare at a young age. I'm not saying this to judge people who make this choice or find they have to do this in order to make a living; however, my husband and I made a conscious decision that our family life was the most important factor to us.

Our journey has not been easy just because we determined to go this way mindfully and purposely. I have lost three babies in the time I've been self-employed. I have cried at 3am worrying about growing credit card bills, wondering how the mortgage would be paid. All the more reason, though, to put profit at the heart of these principles.

Running a business *profitably* as well as *enjoyably* is one of the reasons I wanted to write this book. To give you the tools and knowledge you need to do this yourself. Too many women fall off the proverbial 'glass cliff' after having children. I say it doesn't have to be this way! You have skills, expertise and passion. Use what I share in this book to create your own tiny-time business and make profit super important.

When I speak with prospective clients and they tell me that money is not important to them, yet in the same breath, they want to work with me but can't afford it, the irony is not lost on me or them. Money gives you choices. Hang-ups about money will be reflected in the success of your business. If you make your decisions from a lack mentality, you will attract similarly minded clients. If you believe people won't pay, that you're too expensive or that you're being greedy and taking advantage of people, this will be reflected in your reality.

Getting to grips with money in your business and life is essential if you want the business to work. This is not to say the other principles are not important. Think of the Tiny Time Big Results methodology like a sandwich: Purpose and Play are the bread; Profit and Productivity are the filling. Without a tasty filling, you just have bread. And without the bread, you have a big mess!

Let's get started...

CHAPTER 10: THE BIG FIVE

If you want to have a profitable business in 20 hours a week, there are five core problems that could hold you back. I see business owners struggle with these all the time. I struggled with them too. If you can relate to these, I want you to know you are not alone. I have done every single one of them, and much to my chagrin, I did them for a long time. Until I realised they were holding me back...

If you're doing one, two or all of these, don't worry. I have your back. Soon I'll show you how to stop and replace them with what works!

1. THE REPELLENT MARKETING MESSAGE

One of the big challenges I see regularly with business owners at networking events, conferences and in sales conversations is the inability to articulate what it is they do in clear, compelling and specific language.

If you're struggling to attract clients and income consistently, the first thing you need to look at is your marketing message.

- Is it bland?
- Is it generic?
- Is it vague?
- Is it full of jargon?

If you introduce yourself as a life coach, accountant, business coach, health coach, a social media manager, a marketing strategist or you call yourself a 'ninja' of your industry, your marketing message lacks punch and needs work.

Because it doesn't do what a marketing message should, which is tell people what you do and who you do it for. The message needs to *magnetise* your ideal client and *repel* your nightmare client. Your message needs to capture the attention of your ideal client; as soon as they hear it, they should want to know more. It must intrigue them, increase their curiosity and draw them in.

2. THE DISCONNECTED MARKETING STRATEGY

Would you describe your marketing strategy as deliberate, planned-out and thought-through? Created with the end in mind? Or is it more like throwing spaghetti at the wall and hoping it sticks? Some of the spaghetti might stick, but eventually it all falls off and leaves a mess. Do you sit down at your desk and wonder how to tell people what you're doing? The odd social media post here, a random video there.

If there's no joined-up thinking behind your marketing, it's like chucking all your content out into the void and crossing your fingers that it does something. Without a clear idea what that 'something' even is.

You need clarity around what you're offering and the outcome you want. In order to market that offer successfully, you'll need to reverse-engineer it. That means beginning with the end in mind and determining the steps people need to take in order for them to come to the conclusion they need to buy your stuff!

3. FAILURE TO CONVERT

Marketing and sales are two distinct activities in your business. Marketing lets people know what you do. Sales is how the money from their pocket reaches yours! From my experience and working with my clients, I discovered a huge emphasis on marketing, but so many people were losing sales when it came to the conversion journey. The journey from giving away free content to becoming a paid client.

Sales has a bad reputation (though it is slowly changing). I find most business owners don't identify themselves as sales people. The truth is we are all sales people. We are all always selling our ideas, thoughts, perspectives and views. I am constantly selling to my children — *brush your teeth, eat your dinner, no more biscuits!* Selling is part of how we operate.

At the beginning, I was averse to the idea of selling too. My past experience led me to believe you were foisting your product or service onto poor unsuspecting people and doing them a disservice. Taking their money from them. Some people even feel a huge amount of guilt accepting payment! (This isn't one I'm familiar with personally. I'm perfectly happy receiving my money!)

The fact is making sales is how you bring money into your business. Without sales, you don't have a business. If you're waking up at 3am worrying about the bills and you have a negative view of sales, it's time for change.

The other dimension to this challenge is that you know you need to make sales, but you're terrible at it! You hate the thought of doing a sales conversation, you feel sick in your stomach when you have appointments booked in, and you will do whatever it takes to avoid speaking to someone to try to convert them from interested lead into a paying customer. You might get sick beforehand and cancel the call. When they go to rebook, you put them off. You make it hard for people to book time with you. Booking form well-hidden on your website? Yep, that's another nifty sales avoidance trick.

Failing to convert prospects into paying clients is a business killer and it's one of the chronic challenges facing business owners.

But not now you have this book in your hands! We're about to fix that!

4. TIME-THIRSTY PACKAGES, PROGRAMS AND SERVICES

If you only have 20 hours a week (or less) for your business, not all 20 hours will be billable. Running your own business means you have client work, marketing, sales conversations, administration like filing, tracking your money and so on. Using a conservative estimate, 10 out of the 20 hours will be billable.

This creates a problem if you sell your time, because you don't have much of it! If you can only 'sell' 10 hours of your time and each hour is worth $100, your income potential will be capped at $1000 per week. If you need to make more money, your default logic will be to sell more time, but if you don't have any more time, you're left with no options to make any more money. Packages, programs and services that suck up your time are useless to you if you want a healthy business in just 20 hours a week!

5. TIME SLIPPAGE

As a mother of three, I know only too well how hard it can be to fit everything into your schedule. Therefore, if you only have a few hours to work in your business, it follows that you would know how to be focused. If only it always worked out like that!

Time slippage describes the phenomenon that happens when you sit down to work and you get engrossed and discover an hour has flown by. But you weren't even doing the work that counts. You got sucked into your social media feed, you replied to non-urgent and unimportant emails, and you surfed the net. Social media, email and the internet are prime examples of how we get distracted.

Not knowing *what* to focus on is the bigger issue. If you sit down to work and you don't know what to work on, this is a symptom of a great problem at play. We will address this later on.

Now we know what the five big problems are, let's solve them and get you on the path to profit!

Failing to convert prospects into paying clients is a business killer and it's one of the chronic challenges facing business owners. But not now you have this book in your hands! We're about to fix that!

SECTION 3: THE PURPOSE PRINCIPLE

You can only become truly accomplished at something you love. Don't make money your goal. Instead, pursue the things you love doing, and then do them so well that people can't take their eyes off you.

— Maya Angelou

When you have tiny time, you need something to drive you and move you forward. For some people, it's money but money only takes you so far. When you have purpose and heart behind what you do, you can go the distance. You have a business that makes your heart and purse sing!

CHAPTER 11: YOUR PURPOSE

Why does your business exist? What's it all for? What difference do you believe you are here to make? Purpose is the reason behind everything. Purpose is the thread interwoven through all you do. Purpose comes through in your marketing, your pricing, the way you work — all of it. And it's not to be taken lightly for that reason.

In this section, we're going to dive deep into the purpose of your business.

YOUR WHY

I run my own business because I wanted to create flexibility and freedom, and to have time with my family. I wanted to make a contribution to this world. I wanted to do my bit to push humanity forward. And I wanted to empower myself and others to get control over their money.

I grew up in a culture where, if you were a woman, you left your parents' home to go to your husband's home.

The idea that you would need to find a good (wealthy) husband was drilled into us girls at a young age. I struggled with that concept. Why could I not be in charge of my own financial destiny? Why did I have to rely on someone else?

When you take away a person's financial agency, you are left with dependency and that dependency has always terrified me. I have seen too many examples of men, women and children in terrible situations because of money issues. Which is why it has always been part of my big vision to empower people to learn how to turn their skills, experience and passion into money in the bank. To be self-reliant and self-sufficient. To be in control of their own future and free to make their own choices. It's what I am teaching my children so they are never reliant on someone else or a company or a job for their financial wellbeing.

So what's driving you? What's your purpose? What do you stand for? Why do you want to have your own business? How do you wish to make the world a better place?

This isn't about having a grand notion that you're going to save the world. That kind of thinking can trip you up before your idea even gets a real shot at success. It's about knowing what keeps you going, even on the days that aren't so great.

Here's what I wrote when I posted my 'why' on my social media feed:

I stand for freedom... freedom to live the way you want to live, freedom to spend time with your family, freedom to do the work you want to do. Ultimately the freedom to be who you are meant to be. And to say what you are here to say.

Every significant milestone in my life has been about choosing freedom over conformity. Choosing to move away from home to go to university when it was not the 'done' thing to do, marrying the love of my life when it was not the 'done' thing to do, raising our children the way we see fit even if it doesn't 'fit' into what everyone else does, creating a legacy in my business and making it stand for something.

I stand for freedom.

Now it's your turn. Why are you creating this business? Why did you start it? What do you stand for? What lights you up?

The more you can incorporate **you** into your business, the more powerful and potent it will be.

HOW TO FIND YOUR BUSINESS SWEET SPOT

A business is a way for you to create value in the world and be paid for it. You could be making something, selling your services, selling your expertise, or all of the above! Bringing together what you're good at, your passions, what the world needs and what people will pay for creates a powerful business.

What does your business do? How does it help people? How do you want to help people? Who do you want to serve?

**WHAT YOU'RE GOOD AT + YOUR PASSION + A REAL NEED +
WHAT PEOPLE WILL PAY FOR
= THE SWEET SPOT**

If you're not sure of the answers or even if you think you are, let's go through these four factors now. Been in business a while? This sweet spot activity is a great one to redo every 12 months to keep you fresh and inspired.

Step 1 — GOOD AT

You have talents, skills, expertise and experience. Think about your whole career — everything you have done that has brought you to this point.

List out all the jobs you've ever had, starting from your Saturday job in the local supermarket. (I used to love working on the cash registers!) Keep going until you have exhausted your memory.

Think about all the experience you have gained, the skills you have learnt, the knowledge you have acquired.

Think about what lit you up when working in those jobs and fields. (One of my dream jobs early on was as a training co-ordinator. I love to organise and I got to do it all day long! It was so fulfilling.)

When you start to grow a business — a business that is fulfilling and profitable — make sure you are using all of **you** to make it thrive.

Being a lover of all things planning, spreadsheets and systemising, I incorporate all these into my business and client work. If a client wants me to help them create and deliver their online program, I have my spreadsheet ready to plot it all out. Most of the time, they hate doing this kind of granular work, but I love it, so I make this a valuable selling point!

Step 2 — PASSIONATE ABOUT

What are you passionate about? What are you always talking about? What does that little whisper in your heart say to you?

What do you think is your 'calling'? Why are you here?

When you are daydreaming about what your life could be like and what you could be doing, these are your signposts. Don't ignore them! Journal about them. Write them down. Your soul is speaking to you and these are your goddess winks. Pay attention!

Part of my big dream is travelling the world with my family, sharing my Tiny Time message, running luxury retreats and having a great time. Even if you're not doing it right now, hold fast to the vision!

Step 3 — REALLY NEEDED

Doing what you love doesn't necessarily bring in money. This myth is continually perpetuated, which is frustrating, because I see so many people lose heart when their business idea doesn't work out in practice. 'Build it and they will come' is terrible advice that only worked for Kevin Costner in *A Field of Dreams*. There has to be a real need.

This is a step that a lot of people (including myself) like to skip over, because it feels too much like hard work! But it is crucial, because it's about validating your idea to make sure there is a market need out there. In short... are people looking for this? If someone says to me 'no-one else is doing this' — usually with great enthusiasm at their unique idea — that rings alarm bells for me. If no-one's doing it, that indicates there's no market for it. This isn't always true but people or businesses that do something 'no-one else is doing' are the exceptions, not the norm.

Do your research, talk to people, hang out in online forums, stake out Facebook groups where your ideal client spends time and see what people are talking about. Validate your idea before you pour time and effort into your plan. A simple tweak may be all that stands between you and huge success!

Step 4: WILL PEOPLE PAY?

Whether you charge £100 or £10,000 for your service or product, it doesn't matter. If the market you serve is not willing to pay, you will always struggle. Your business will not build traction, nor will it gain momentum.

This is where niching down to a specific group is so powerful. You could have an amazing weight-loss process that creates mind-blowing transformations. But if you're aiming it at students who don't have two pennies to rub together, it won't work. If you aim it at the high flier corporate executive who is always traveling and worries about the weight they're gaining, you will find it much easier to sell your service.

Find the people who will pay for what you offer and do your pro-bono work on the side. But make sure you are sustained in your business. Feed and clothe yourself so you can continue your work!

WHAT IS YOUR MESSAGE?

Do you have a message? You might not think you do, but when you communicate with your audience about your business, you will need a message to share with them.

It's not about having a grand message, where you hope to cure world poverty and stop wars. (This isn't a beauty pageant!) Your message is about what is *important to you* and to the people you are here to serve.

What's important to you and what's important to them? Here are some examples to inspire your thinking:

- Carpenter? You create beauty for people's homes.
- Run a health food shop? You empower people to make better choices about their food.
- Hairdresser? You inspire confidence in your clients.
- Dating coach? You cure loneliness.
- Money coach? You teach powerful money habits so people don't get into bad debt.
- Accountant? You teach business owners how to keep more of their money (legally).
- Mindfulness teacher? You inspire calm in anxious children.

My message is focused on financial freedom, fulfilling work, loved ones spending time together, connecting and loving life fully, with the money and time to enjoy it.

What is your message?

Journal your answers in the workbook, which you can get here. www.yasminvorajee.com/jointtbookclub/

WHO DO YOU WANT TO SERVE?

Who do you feel called to serve in your business? Is there a particular group of people you feel pulled towards? Or perhaps someone you've worked with in the past who was an absolute dream to work with and whose outcomes were superb?

Identifying your ideal client is the bedrock of all business. And I find it is one of the questions that creates the most confusion and angst for business owners. For some, it can take years (and tears) to nail.

There are over 7 billion people in the world. Your business does not rely on you working with all of those people. There will be people who will benefit *most* from what you do. There will be a group of people who will get the fastest results from what you do. There will be people you would hate to work with. For example, if your business is focused on clean eating and health, you may abhor the idea of working with someone who regularly eats fast food. Or if you work with the corporate market, you may dread the idea of working with companies that don't have a strong social corporate responsibility approach. You may love working with women. Or you may only want to work with men.

It's not about excluding people. It's about creating a clear image of who you want to work with. When it comes to identifying this group for your business, focus on the **problems** they face, the **values** they hold, what they **aspire** to and what they **fear**.

Too often, businesses start creating products, programs and services without a clear idea of who they are for. Then they try to market to everybody. They will try to dominate all the social media channels, go to every networking event, and advertise wherever they can. The problem is this leads to burnout. You burn out yourself, your time and your money. This approach requires deep pockets!

Narrowing down your focus enables you to be far more targeted with your marketing. Understanding your audience fully allows you to create the exact program or service they need, as opposed to guessing.

When you know who they are, you then listen to what they are saying. How do they describe their problems — in their own words? Clarity in this area does not come from your head! It comes from listening to your potential audience.

I am constantly researching what my market is looking for. In conversations with prospects, on social media, in opinion forums, in the media. I want to know what they are saying, the exact words they use that I can incorporate into my marketing material. Many business owners are cursed with too much knowledge, often making the mistake of speaking to their customers in the same way they speak about their expertise. Never is it more important to use the words of your ideal client than when you are sharing your message and you want them to hear it.

The key thing with narrowing your focus means you know who you want to work with and the people you don't. I will not work with people who aren't ready to take action. People who are quick to make excuses instead of focusing on the work. People who are not open. People who believe they know everything and have tried everything. People who are in business solely to make money.

Remember, in your marketing, you want to attract your ideal client and repel the client you don't want. You cannot serve everybody. Indeed, when you try to work with everybody, you end up working with nobody! Businesses thrive when they narrow their focus. It may feel counterintuitive and restrictive at times. But when you narrow your focus, your marketing is far more detailed, specific and targeted at the right people. Now you can find your audience more easily.

And this strategy gets bonus points, because it saves you a tremendous amount of time. You don't have to be on all social media. You don't have to be advertising in a paper that none of your ideal clients read. You can identify the magazines, the newspapers, the industry publications, the networking events, the conferences and the online channels that work best for your ideal client. You identify who they are and where they spend time. You insert yourself there and you start the conversation. When you do this, you grow your audience and your business.

You may resist this advice because you believe you will narrow your market and limit your options. Be assured the complete opposite happens. When you narrow your focus, you become known for serving a particular group of people. Your business grows and you can spread your wings.

But you can't do this until you build enough momentum.

Key questions to ask to identify your ideal client:

- What problem do I solve for them?
- Who do I love working with?
- Who can I get a result for fast?
- Does this group know they have a problem?
- Are they looking for a solution?
- Are they willing to pay?
- What is different about this group than others?
- What are their aspirations and fears?
- Why would they gravitate to me and not someone else?

These questions are also in your workbook:
www.yasminvorajee.com/jointtbookclub/

WHAT DO YOU WANT TO BE KNOWN FOR?

What do you stand for? What would you like to be known for? Do you want to become renowned for your passion for helping people embrace the vegan lifestyle? Or finding the love of their life? Do you want people to describe you as warm, generous, hard-hitting, stylish, humorous, confident or with a ballsy attitude?

Your brand is bigger than the colours of your website or your logo. Those are representations of your brand but they are not your brand. How you show up in the world, your message, how you interact with your audience and how you serve your clients reflects you, your values and how you want to be seen. It must be in alignment with who you are internally. You can't fool people into thinking you're someone you're not — you'll get caught out in no time!

YOUR BIG PICTURE

When I talk about a 20-hour week business, some people dismiss the idea and declare it impossible. After all, there are many podcasts, videos and 'gurus' who insist you need to work 100+ hours a week before your business can be successful. This is where creating your own definition of success is crucial. My definition of success does not include working long hours. I measure my success in terms of results, not hours spent.

In my world, I already have a job that I never switch off from; it's called parenting! I want the business and parenting to co-exist in harmony. I don't want my business to take precious time from my babies, but I also love the business because it keeps me sane! I desire quality of life too, which means doing what I love, with the people I adore, and getting to enjoy it all.

What's your definition of success? Your definition has to resonate with you.

When I was starting out, a coach asked me my monthly income goal. When I told her 3k, her response was: "Is that all?" In one fell swoop, my heart sank and my passion deflated. She accused me of aiming too low and not having a big enough vision. But that was my number, the number that made me feel abundant and expansive.

Irrespective of whether it's 3k a month, 10k or 50k, your number is your number. You know how much money you want in order to be able to create the life you want. Own that number and be proud of it!

The next step is to create crystal clarity around what you want to achieve through your business, and most importantly, how your business fits in with your life.

Here are some questions you need to answer to create your exciting big picture:

- How many hours do you want to work?
- How much money do you want to make?
- How do you want to work with your clients?
- How many weeks a year do you want to work?
- How many holidays will you take off?
- Do you want to have a team?
- Will you have premises?

You can answer these in the workbook to help you create clarity and your big picture.

THE PURPOSE PRINCIPLE IN A NUTSHELL

Congratulations! Well done on getting this far, and putting in the work and thought. Like everything in life, you get out what you put in. Remember to use the accompanying workbook to jot down your ideas — it's powerful to write down what comes to mind rather than having a myriad of thoughts swimming around in your head! It can get noisy in there, but when you write it down, calm descends!

With your purpose front and centre, you have a great foundation for your business to thrive, but remember to keep revisiting this as you grow. It's not something you do once and forget. It's key to review your motivations at each stage of your business.

The Purpose Principle is about having:

- A clear purpose for your business
- A compelling vision of what you want to be known for
- A business that plays to your sweet spot of experience, knowledge and expertise
- A magnetic big picture
- A strong statement that outlines **what** you do and **who** you do it for

Next, we'll move to that all-important principle of profit. Let's get you making more money!

SECTION 4: THE PROFIT PRINCIPLE

Making money is art and working is art and good business is the best art.

— Andy Warhol

This section is all about the money! There's a good reason why I talk so much about having a profitable business in your 20 hours a week. You don't need years of experience in business or a PhD to know that making money is critical. It's the fuel in your engine. It keeps everything moving. It also stops you from waking up at 3am worrying about bills and how you're going to pay off the credit card (which I am sad to say, I did a lot).

Yet it was only when I was working with my clients that I realised how many people start businesses feeling adrift when it comes to looking at the money. And in many cases, business owners avoid it point blank!

But knowing your numbers is essential. Money can be an emotive issue for so many — I get why people avoid looking at their numbers — but if we strip away the emotion, we can make a lot more progress. That's why, when people ask me about how to better manage their time, I know time poverty is merely a symptom of the issue, not the cause. When you have a **solid business model** and you know how to work it to get a great return, time management is no longer a problem.

To reach this stage, you need to take time out to focus on how you make money to ensure you're doing the right things at the right time, not wasting time on projects and products that are not creating a strong enough return.

What I cover in this section is the curriculum for my program, the Tiny Time Business School. I'm about to show you **what** you need to know and **why** you need to know it. I cover some of the **how** here, but as you can imagine, technology and trends change quickly. The whole point of this book is to give you the principles. If you want to dive deeper into the exact path that you should take, the Tiny Time Business School program will show you how. This approach ensures what I teach is as up-to-date as possible. Rest assured, the underlying principles remain the same.

As this is a chunky section, here is an overview of what we'll be covering so you can see how it maps out.

Having a profitable business in 20 hours a week means you focus on four core areas:

PART 1: MESSAGE — *A punchy, specific and compelling marketing message.*

PART 2: LEVERAGE — *Products, programs and services that are scalable, profitable and enjoyable to deliver.*

PART 3: ATTRACTION — *A cohesive marketing strategy that brings in a consistent flow of high-quality leads.*

PART 4: CONVERSION — *Simple and proven ways to turn prospects into buyers gracefully.*

When you break the four core areas down, it translates into nine distinct steps. Keep this in mind as you read this section and refer back to this overview if you're not sure how it all fits together.

1. Craft an irresistible marketing message
2. Create a compelling signature program
3. Design a lead magnet and short-term nurture sequence
4. Create your six-month marketing, content and conversion calendar
5. Get appointment-ready
6. Raise your conversion rate
7. On-board and delight your clients
8. Manage your time and energy
9. Mind your mindset

Steps 8 and 9 will be covered under the Productivity and Play principles.

PROFIT PRINCIPLE PART 1: MESSAGING

CHAPTER 12: THE WHAT AND THE WHO

I can trace the hardest and leanest times in my business back to when I knew nothing about what I did for my clients. Since I didn't know what I did, I couldn't articulate it to the people I wanted to reach.

Your marketing message is one of the most important foundations of your business. If you don't have a marketing message that stands out for your ideal client, you will struggle in your business and it will feel like you're climbing Mount Everest *every single day*. Curiously, a lot of business owners don't see why it's so important and why they should be focused on it.

When I work with clients, I ask them to tell me their 'elevator pitch'. I know, you're probably cringing right now. Either you hate the idea of an elevator pitch altogether or you have one that just doesn't cut it. That's okay — we're going to work on this now!

Love it or hate it, the elevator pitch is here to stay. But take the sting out of it and realise it's a powerful tool for you to communicate what you do and who you do it for.

Events, conferences and networking events are opportunities for you to wow your potential clients, collaborators and referrers, but you have just a 30 to 60 second window to impress someone — not with your achievements or your ego — but with searing clarity about what you do. Talk about tiny time!

For too long, I struggled with this. I created bland and vague titles and descriptions of what I did for people. This meant I made no money! And it's exactly why I get evangelical about making sure you don't make the same mistake! Your business message — the umbrella concept of what you do — has to be specific. It needs to magnetise the people you are here to serve. It must repel the 'wrong' people. If we were comparing it to ice-cream, it can't be vanilla. It needs to be tutti-frutti or pistachio! Something that makes it stand out. When someone hears your message, they need to know it is 100% for them or 100% not.

This is where the work on your ideal client is crucial, because you could be the most amazing weight loss coach in the country, but unless you are specific about exactly who it's for, the message won't land.

We covered this briefly earlier in the Purpose Principle, but as it's an integral part of your business, let's dig deeper now. Without a clear message, you won't attract your ideal clients who will pay for your services, your program or your packages.

There are a number of ways you can figure out your message. My favoured approach is to focus on the problem they struggle with. For example, here's my message:

I help business owners run a profitable business in 20 hours a week or less. I work with people who have the problem of limited time.

When you focus on a problem, your job is to then create a solution. Doing so allows you to go deep into a specific area and build solid momentum. The beauty of this approach means, if you are clear on the problems your ideal client struggles with and you can articulate them well, that prospective client will believe you have the solution for them. And they will buy!

An inch wide, a mile deep.

This piece of advice has stayed with me for years when it comes to niching. There are plenty of examples where people are marketing to 'everybody', but the key thing to remember is they did not start that way. Maybe they have mass appeal now, but did you know Tony Robbins started out curing phobias, Gary Vaynerchuk started out with his family's wine business, and Amy Porterfield started out teaching Facebook? These are examples of successful people in my industry. There are probably lots of examples in yours.

Start specific, build and grow this narrowly focused business, then you can think about evolving and doing more. But when you have tiny time, the key focus is what you can do in the time you have. If you try to wear too many hats, it is a recipe for disaster.

What vs How

One of the common mistakes I see is confusing **what** you do with **how** you do it. If you run retreats as part of your business and someone asks what you do, the answer is not 'I run retreats'. What do you do on the retreats? Do you run digital detox retreats? Self-care retreats? Business planning retreats? Health and wellbeing retreats? See the difference? Go back to your message and make sure you are 100% clear on what you do for your people.

The idea behind a compelling marketing message or your 60-second elevator pitch is to invite more conversation. You want the person to ask you for more information. You won't make a sale in that 60-second window, but if you intrigue them, if you create a curiosity and reel them in, you've opened up a bigger conversation. Not everybody will be your ideal client. However, they will usually know someone else who fits the description, someone who could be a great referral source for you, or someone to connect you to for a collaboration.

Remember, you want to stand out. You want to be memorable!

Here's a handy format for you to formulate your statement:

I help ....
(INSERT IDEAL CLIENT)

to ....
(SOLVE THEIR PROBLEM)

so they can ....
(THE RESULT/OUTCOME)

I wrote this in an earlier section but it bears repeating because it's so important! At the basis of any magnetic marketing message is knowing who you work with and who you're targeting. I encourage you to have a piece of paper with your statement of **what you do** and **who you do it for** in front of you all the time. Refer back to this constantly during your work. Create an image in your head of this person, give her a name and direct everything you do this person. Every email you type, every video you post, and every blog you write, every product you create, every service you design... you get the gist!

PROFIT PRINCIPLE PART 2: LEVERAGE

CHAPTER 13: THE MAGIC OF LEVERAGE

What exactly is leverage and why is it critical to a tiny-time business? A basic definition of leverage relates to a lever as a tool for getting more work done with less physical force. To illustrate, imagine you have a flat tyre. You can't lift the car up with your bare hands to replace the tyre. It's too heavy. But if you use a jack to raise the car up enough, you can easily change the tyre. The jack is your leverage.

In a tiny-time business, leverage is your best friend. It's allows you to amplify your time and resources so you can create the results you want like revenue and impact. For example a VIP or **premium program** is a way to create leverage because it creates a highly desired outcome, but you base the price of it on the value to the client, not the amount of time it takes. This allows you to leverage your time and make a great income. Similarly, you create an **online course** once and sell it again and again. This allows you to leverage your time and make money repeatedly from one course. Leverage in your marketing could look like taking one blog post and using it in several ways (e.g. as video, as text, as audio).

We'll be talking about leverage throughout the book because it's essential in a tiny-time business.

How to Build Leverage in a Tiny-Time Business

My approach to building leverage in your business is to create your signature program, product or service, which embodies the work you do, and using this program, product or service as the foundation of your business. You can use your **signature program** as the basis of all your offers, programs, services, your marketing, your talks and your webinars. You can also build leverage into your sales process, how you use your time, how you manage your money and how you nurture your wellbeing through simple processes and routines. Leverage is that powerful and that's what I'll show you.

The first step is to create your signature program. There are five steps to doing this. In this part of the Profit Principle, we will go through each one.

1. Promise
2. Process
3. Package
4. Price
5. Leveraged streams of income

I have mapped out this process in your workbook so be sure to download it from the Book Club resources page so you can follow along. Join the Tiny Time Book Club here: www.yasminvorajee.com/jointtbookclub/

CHAPTER 14: YOUR SIGNATURE PROGRAM

THE PROMISE

Once you have established what you do and who you do it for, it's time to create clarity on how you do this. When you have tiny time, you need to be clear on your money-makers and focus on them to help you generate a healthy income. One of my early clients Laura had an eBook on how to use LinkedIn. It was priced at 99 cents and she wanted to make an income of $3k per month. When I asked how many she needed to sell, she looked sheepish and said, "About 3,000". In that moment, a lightbulb went off. She repeated what she'd just realised, then looked at me and said, "What was I thinking?!" She had a list of 150 people and she was looking to sell 3,000 copies a month of her book to create her desired income. At that moment, she knew she had work to do. I walked her through the concept that I am now going to take you through.

First of all, get clear on the transformation you create for people.

What is the end result that someone will achieve as a result of working with you? What do you promise them?

- Will they lose weight?

- Will they be a great manager?
- Will they land their dream job?
- Will they find their dream partner?
- Will they be able to sell their home with minimum fuss?
- Will they know how to organise the money in the business and minimise their tax liability?
- Will they know how to get their kids to sleep through the night?
- Will they be able to get their kids to eat all their veggies?
- Will they land those corporate contracts?
- Will they write their book?

Get clear on the transformation and the promise. *Hint: This will become a major part of your marketing message!*

Next comes the process...

THE PROCESS

If someone chooses to work with you, they believe you can help them to create a specific result. You will go on to take them through a process that takes them from A to B.

By articulating your process and breaking it down now, you will understand clearly how to package the transformation you provide. But be warned! This is where the curse of too much knowledge kicks in. The trick is not giving them too much industry talk and putting it in terms they will identify with. What you do for others comes easily to you so you may find it hard to break down the process. To combat this, I recommend finding a friend to help you clarify your thinking. Ideally, choose someone who knows little about what you do and explain how you take a customer through the process. This is what I call your **signature process**.

It's the core of how you do what you do.

Let's look at an example. Say you're a dating coach and you specialise in helping people with online dating. Your process takes them from creating their online profile to choosing the best picture, understanding how to find people to connect with to making contact and so on.

Another example is my own business. When somebody works with me in the Tiny Time Business School program, I have a clear process that focuses on the four core areas I talk about in this book:

- Message
- Leverage
- Attraction
- Conversion

Using these headings, I break down the process into nine detailed steps, each of which helps my clients create a streamlined and simplified business that means they attract clients and cash consistently, and can grow and scale their business with ease. In 20 hours a week or less.

When you know how many steps you have, it allows you to determine what kind of program, package or service you will create. Which leads us to the next question. How will you bring it all together into a package?

THE PACKAGE

If your process has seven steps, is it a seven-week program? Or seven months? Maybe a self-study course with seven modules? Your transformation process could take five steps, maybe fewer, maybe more. I wouldn't advise that you have fewer than three steps. If you do, look to see if you can break down those steps further.

What comes easily to you will not come easily to your client, so your steps need to be as clear and simple as possible to prevent overwhelm and confusion for your client. At the same time, you don't want to have a process that has 21 steps. Too many steps can be overpowering. Remember, you don't have to include everything. Less is more when you're designing a signature program.

As you do this work, keep asking yourself the question: *what is the result I am promising?*

Once you have outlined your process and determined the number of steps, you then need to decide how you will deliver this program. This is where many business owners fight the temptation to pack everything into their program, including the kitchen sink! Restraint is key here as there is a balance to strike between wanting to create a fantastic program or service and overwhelming your client with giving them too much.

If your signature program or service has seven steps, decide the timeframe for the program and how you will work with the client to create the transformation. Will the program be delivered through a series of calls, a series of one-day workshops, an online course accompanied by private coaching calls, or delivered solely via email?

If you're an accountant, do you do your client's annual tax return? Is your package solely focused on the tax return or do you offer quarterly meetings as well to add value?

If you're a healthy eating coach, your package might include a series of calls and private mentoring days where you shop for food with them and show them how to cook healthy meals from scratch.

If you're a coach for high-achieving corporate women, your package might include a series of calls, days with you and email support.

When deciding the delivery details for your program or service, think about your ideal client, the experience you want to create for them and what excites you! What feels interesting and fun to you is a crucial part of the decision-making process. If you don't enjoy the delivery of your program or service, you will get bored and won't do your best work. Your client will suffer as a result.

To create an amazing rock-solid signature program or service, my recommendation is to do this work with your clients on a one-on-one basis first. Before you decide to create an online program or course, you need to be sure your process creates the transformation your client desires. The only way to do this is through experience. My process has changed considerably in the last 18 months and it was only by doing this work with clients that I could refine and hone my Tiny Time Business School signature program. Which meant when it came to re-writing this book, it was much easier for me and I was able to write 35,000 words in one month.

When you do this work with one-on-one clients, you pick up on nuances and subtleties that you wouldn't have otherwise. They are not inconsequential. These nuances and subtleties make you and your program unique and help you stand out from the crowd.

Some examples of signature programs for you:

My clients Agne and EJ have a fitness gym. They promote a 90-day program to help people lose weight and keep it off.

My client Mary creates beautiful bespoke wedding lingerie. The transformation is luxurious shapewear you can wear even with the most daring of backs or necklines!

My client Kate has a program for eating well when you have hypothyroidism.

My client Padraig teaches how to focus your mind in 90-minute bursts, which works brilliantly for students.

All these clients offer other products and services, but these are their signature programs.

Now let's price it!

THE PRICE

One of the questions I ask in sales conversations is how much my clients want to make from their business. As I said at the start, I'm always astounded when I hear 'I'm not motivated by money' for the reasons I mentioned above, notably that money matters. (Remember the chickens!) Interestingly, I never ask: how do you feel about money? I always ask: how much do you want to make?

In a tiny-time business, you must put aside the emotional factors and be clear how much you want to make. This will help you to determine your pricing decisions and how many clients you need to hit your goal. It also means you will establish goalposts. When you hit those goals, you'll know it! And that means you can allow yourself to celebrate and not simply move the goalposts and start working towards the next goal.

Please take the time to do the sums for your business. If you want a monthly income of 3k and your core offer is 500, you need to sell six items. If your core offer is 1k, you need to sell three items. If your monthly income target is 5k, you adjust your figures accordingly.

Later in this section when we discuss sales, you will see just how important it is to be clear on which numbers you need to keep a close eye on in your business.

There are five factors to take into account with pricing:

1. Cost of Business

To have a strong pricing strategy, you have to ensure your costs are covered. So if you sell a product or service for £100 and your costs are £46, you will make £54. If you sell for £46, you're breaking even. We don't want to break even. We want to make a profit. Even if you sold your product at £50, you would still make a profit. This leads me onto the cost of doing business.

To set up a business today (particularly one where you sell your expertise) requires a lot less investment than previously. A great website doesn't cost the earth and your cost of entry can be low through the savvy use of social media. But just because your costs may be low doesn't mean you must automatically charge a lower price.

2. Income Goals

How much do you want to make? Are you clear on the figure? When pricing, take into account your income goals and compare that to the number of sales you expect to make. If you price your program or service too low, you won't reach your income target.

3. Value

If people balk at your price tag, it is because you have not articulated the value of it clearly enough. If you have a program that helps someone find the love of their life, reflect the value in your pricing. If you help someone feel like a million dollars in their wedding dress, reflect this in your price.

Base your prices on the value of what you're offering, never on your worth. I have never agreed with the idea that I should 'charge my worth'. You couldn't afford me... I'm priceless. And so are you!

Don't charge your worth, charge the value of your offer! And most importantly, **believe** in the value of what you are offering! If you don't, who will?

4. Positioning

Recently, my eldest son and I were out shopping and were looking at the tinned tomatoes section. There were at least three choices. The supermarket's own value brand (the cheapest), the mid-priced options and the 'premium' or 'luxury sun-dried Mediterranean' option, which was the most expensive. "You should get that one, Mum," my son said, "It's the most expensive. It must be the best."

Pricing is a positioning tool. The psychology of pricing means most people are likely to think the most expensive option is the best option. It's not always true but this is how our brains process information. If you price too low, your buyer may be put off because they perceive it as too low to provide the value you claim.

5. Money Hang-ups

Pricing can be emotive but it need not be. I find it common for people to undercharge. They don't take account of their costs and end up walking away with little to nothing.

Instead of taking a deliberate and methodical approach to pricing, you may be basing your price on your own hang-ups around money. Perhaps you charge too little because you don't have a lot of money right now and you use your own circumstances to reflect your business offering. Or you believe your ideal client doesn't have the money.

To overcome this, look at the internal dialogue that occurs when you decide your price for your offer. Is there a little voice saying it's too expensive or that no-one will buy? When I price my offers, I like to feel into them and get aligned with the price internally to ensure there is no conflict. I do this through simple meditation and allowing my inner wisdom to bubble up. You will know when you hit the right price for you. You may still have some niggles about charging what you want to charge and that's okay. It's normal. What is more important is that you charge a price that feels right for you. With over 7 billion people in the world, you can find the people who will pay, as long as you find the right people and articulate the value to them.

What you don't want to do is let your own money hang-ups dictate your income potential. If you struggle with pricing and you know you're holding yourself back, do something about it. Work with a coach and get to the bottom of this.

My client Cathy was undercharging for her webinars. She charged £5 for a 60-minute webinar. When I told her it was too low for the value she was offering and suggested she charged £20, she felt a lot of resistance so we settled on £12. Here's the best part... She had made zero sales at £5. When she put the price up to £12, she sold 10 spots! Pricing is all about positioning.

How Do People Come to You?

When I started the business, I was naïve. I didn't think about how people would come to work with me. I had a vague notion that I would talk to people, and by magic, they would want to pay me and all would be well. That approach didn't work out so well and it's not something I'd recommend!

What I do recommend is having a clear path that people take, a path you can signpost for them. If you get paying clients into your business through sales conversations, your focus should be on how you encourage people to book an appointment with you. Is it through your blogs or your videos? Do you hold free open evenings? Do you run workshops? Do you do webinars? Do you run challenges? Is it through search engines? Map out the most common ways people find you and book appointments with you. If these methods work for you and generate a good return on investment, keep doing those.

A few more examples to get you thinking... I run free webinars. At the end of the webinar, I encourage people to book a no-obligation Tiny Time Triage session with me. On my blogs, free videos and podcast, I also ask them to book a call with me. Sales conversations bring in 80% of my business so I focus on getting appointments. Your model may be through a webinar where you sell one-to-many. During the webinar, you make an offer and you sell your program. Be clear on how people come to you and ensure your marketing is aligned to this.

It Takes Time

At this stage, allow me to emphasise again that this is not a linear process. Remember, you will revisit what you do, who you do it for and how you do it a number of times as you test and tweak your business model and how you work. This is 100% normal!

The other thing I say to all my clients without fail is to **be patient!** Doing this work takes time and requires a scientific approach. Think of yourself in a lab, testing what works, trialling your ideas and watching for the results. No scientist would throw in the towel after one day. Everything has a gestation period; if you are too impatient, you will miss out. If you try a marketing method and it doesn't bear fruit after a few days and you switch to another way, you will never know how good it could have been. Simply because you let your impatience take over!

Another way to think of it is by seeing yourself as a gardener. You plant the seeds, you wait for them to flower. You need a gestation period to allow the idea to grow, for you to test it and see if it works, or decide what small tweaks need to be made. Or you could be a farmer like my husband. Farmers know they sow then they reap.

Whether their business is cattle or wheat, nothing worthwhile happens instantly and there are no overnight successes. You may be forgiven for thinking George Clooney was an overnight success after the hit show *ER*. Even he says his overnight success was 20 years in the making!

Everything has a gestation period. If you're too impatient, you'll miss out.

CHAPTER 15: LEVERAGED STREAMS OF INCOME

Trading time for money in a tiny-time business is a fool-proof way to limit your income potential and the growth of your business. It's not something I recommend! One of the pillars of a strong tiny-time business is having leveraged streams of income so you are not selling your time. In this chapter, I'll share with you some of my favourite ways to create leveraged income.

As you read this section, think about how this could work in your business.

PREMIUM SERVICES AND PACKAGES

Creating premium services and packages is one of my favourite ways of establishing a solid income from the start, which helps to take the stress out of daily life.

This is where you create a valuable and value-full package or service around a result your client desires. It's based on value, not time. Time is mostly irrelevant in a premium service or package, but this concept is where a lot of business owners struggle. They want to define the package in terms of hours, rather than value. When it comes to services you can charge a premium for 'done for you' or 'done with you' service. Or you could deliver a two-hour session and charge £2000 because you have helped your client create a result that is 10x the investment.

When Marilyn came to work with me, she was running her garden design business in Portugal and was juggling that with raising her 18-month old baby. During our time together, we restructured how she worked by showing how she could add massive value and charge more without her doing the legwork. Her clients want her because she has expertise with plants that don't need a lot of water to thrive, which is perfect for the geographic location where she is based. But she didn't need to be the one digging and planting! A simple mindset shift enabled Marilyn to reclaim her time, spend more time with her family and still make a great income.

Caveat: Premium packages take a specific mindset to deliver. It's not just about adding a zero to your package, program or service. Unless you are congruent in your belief and ability to deliver the premium package, you will not feel comfortable and confident selling it. Your potential client will smell the incongruence and won't buy.

Creating premium services and packages is one of my favourite ways of establishing a solid income from the start, which helps to take the stress out of daily life.

CASE STUDY

How to Go from Selling a £50 Product to a £750 Product and Be Sold Out Months in Advance

When I first met Mary in 2014, she was making beautiful handmade lingerie. It was taking her about eight hours to make one piece. She was charging £50 and only just covering her costs. Add in her time investment and she was making a loss.

Undercharging can happen for a number of reasons. In Mary's case, the main reason was she was not valuing her time or her considerable skill. However, Mary was very open to making changes so her business was profitable without taking up so much time. She wanted more time with her young family and to look after her health.

Through our work together, she decided to stop making the lingerie and instead branch out into creating a premium product. Deciding what that was and taking action did not happen overnight but she is now one of the only creators of specialised tailored bridal shapewear in the world.

Her background as an engineer and her sewing capability made this a dream combination. So now she looks after brides worldwide who want to look spectacular in their dress, especially if they have a plunging back or neckline that means shop-bought shapewear just won't work.

She worked hard to position herself as the go-to person for bridal shapewear. She now makes at least 15x what she used to for one piece, is profiled regularly, and more importantly, books out months in advance. Without working longer hours!

Check out Mary's business at www.siodalingerie.co.uk

DIGITAL ASSETS (ONLINE COURSES, EBOOKS, BOOKS, SHORT COURSES)

When Padraig came to me, he was fully booked in his wellness clinic, but was struggling with his time and income ceiling. He asked me to help him create an online course that would enable him to leverage his time.

During our work together, we co-created his signature program, the one he wants to be known for, called the 90-Minute Focus Method. It became the basis of his online work, even though he did continue his practice. Nearly three years later, he and his program are going from strength to strength.

When you have tiny time, selling time for money is not a sustainable strategy. You have a set amount of time. If you only focus on selling this, you put a ceiling on your income potential. You have to get savvy with what you do to generate revenue. And one of the best ways you can do that is by creating digital assets. This means you create digital products like eBooks, webinars, online courses or workshops that you can sell to many. The key is to create once, sell many times.

Travel is a barrier in my business. Running the business around school runs means I have to be creative with how I deliver my training. The baby is always with me, and because my husband's work is unpredictable, how I work has to be flexible. I started doing online webinars early on in my business and they remain an integral part of how I reach my audience. I have to say, there is nothing quite like waking up in the morning and seeing PayPal notifications telling me I've sold a workshop or a program. There is a hyped-up myth about making money while you sleep. It is possible but you have to know it's not something that happens automatically. There's no such thing as truly passive income. Everything takes attention and effort.

LEVERAGED ASSETS

Building on the concept of digital assets, you can then take it to the next level and create ways to serve many people at the same time.

Online programs, group memberships, workshops or masterminds are all ways you can work with more than one person at a time but not suffer a drop in income. In fact, you can make more money. As a business owner, this leverages your time beautifully.

Note: A mastermind is when a group of business owners and entrepreneurs at similar stages of their business get together to combine their collective skills, knowledge and networks to grow their business. I've run a number of masterminds myself and they are phenomenal for creating momentum!

To give you an example of leveraging, instead of working with private clients one at a time, run a group program with well-structured weekly group sessions. This means if you have 10 people in the group, instead of spending 10 hours a week (or one hour per person), you can schedule a two-hour session and serve everybody together. With this simple strategy, you save eight hours every week.

A group program enables people to learn from each other and creates strong accountability. It also creates laser-focused clients. Often times, we overestimate what we can achieve in a week (especially when we have tiny time) so instead of packing everything into an hour-long call, your client comes prepared to the call with what they need right now.

LEVERAGE MASTERY

This is where business gets really exciting. One of the most powerful things you can do in your tiny-time business is to create multiple streams of income. It's not something that happens overnight, but it is something I want you to work towards. Like everything, though, I don't want you to reinvent the wheel. The approach I favour is to create your core program, your signature program, and turn that into a premium package, an online program and a book, which becomes part of your sales funnel. As you can see, one core program becomes three streams of income.

You take your signature program and make this your sales funnel. Your premium package is the most expensive, the online program (delivered live or sold year-round as 'evergreen') is your mid-priced package and the book is the low-priced offer. You create these one at a time, but essentially you're taking the same core signature program and packaging it into different formats, which all bring in income.

This is a smart way to leverage your knowledge and expertise! Solid ways to make a great income in your tiny-time business.

Now let's look at how you attract your clients.

PROFIT PRINCIPLE PART 3: CLIENT ATTRACTION

CHAPTER 16: WHAT GOOD MARKETING DOES FOR YOU

Marketing is about reducing friction. You are a business owner with a service or product to sell. You want people to buy your stuff! Marketing is the way you let people know about it in a way that leads to a sale.

To do this, you need to reduce friction in the mind of your buyer. People typically need between seven and eleven interactions with you before they will buy, for example, reading your blog, watching your video, reading an email from you, listening to your podcast or hearing you in an interview. It's not just about seeing you on social media the odd time. They want to know they're making a good decision so the aim of your marketing is to reinforce you are worth their time and attention. And as the world gets noisier, they may need a lot more than those eleven interactions in the future.

Why do you need this? You may be familiar with the concept of 'know, like and trust'. People buy from people. They will spend money with you when they are familiar with you, feel a connection to you, have a level of trust. That relationship is where we will be focusing our attention next.

EDUCATION-BASED MARKETING
Marketing has to be a two-way process. It's not just shouting about

your programs and services. It's about starting a conversation with your audience and letting them know who you are, what you do, and most importantly, how you can help them.

Education-based marketing is where you educate your audience on the need for your program or service. When you educate people, you inform them and create a deeper conversation, rather than a simple, crude 'buy my stuff' approach. You educate your audience on the problem you solve for them. You paint a picture of how this impacts their life. The bigger the problem, the more committed they are to finding a solution. Then you show them how it can be resolved.

This is my favourite approach because you get to share why you do what you do, who you are, why you care about them and how you can help them. This also builds on the reciprocity principle which comes from a model about influencing people by author Robert Cialdini. He talks about giving away your information and it creates a relationship. If your audience feels like they're getting great value from you (even if it's all free), they are more likely to stay with you.

Many business owners feel wobbly about giving away their knowledge and are afraid nobody will go on to buy what they offer. This is when your savvy marketing strategy comes into action! When you create a marketing strategy based on what you're offering, you can determine which elements you will give away for free and what people will have to pay for.

A key point to remember is that information is everywhere. We are awash with information, so a lack of information is never the problem. It's how you structure it to help people create the result they want that counts and will get you results.

People will pay for implementation, so don't be afraid of giving away what you know strategically, because your value lies in helping them to implement. That is also where you can charge a premium, one of my favourite ways of creating generous revenue in a tiny-time business. (I may have mentioned this before!)

STORYTELLING MARKETING

Telling stories is an ancient tradition. It's how we teach our children. (Though some fairy tales leave a lot to be desired!) It's also how we communicate with each other. It's how we hold attention and it's how we liven up a boring topic!

Telling stories well is an art form, but don't let that stop you incorporating it into your marketing strategy. A lot of my marketing doesn't feel like marketing. Recently, I did a video on why my slow-cooker is a godsend. I even shared the recipe (lamb with chickpeas, red lentils and spinach), and received an abundance of views and comments on that quick two-minute video. Now, I don't sell slow-cookers in my business but using one is part of my story. A slow-cooker saves me a huge amount of time cooking for my family. It takes me 10 minutes to put the ingredients together and throw it in there. I can have dinner off my mind before 8am, except we're tortured all day with the divine smells from the kitchen! But then at 6pm, we tuck into lamb that is soft like butter. How is this anything to do with my offers? It's not! But it ties in with my brand, which is all about tiny pockets of time and how best to use them. In telling my slow-cooker story, I am sharing my tips and strategies.

I encourage my clients to do the same.

- If you make soap and you're out picking fresh lavender to put into the soap, make a video of it. Share the story of how you lovingly pick the lavender and how it becomes part of your product.

- If you're a nutritionist and you're at the local farmer's market, share your passion for the produce.

- If you're a stylist and you have just seen an amazing dress, do a video about it or take a picture and share it. You're not selling the dress, but you are sharing what you love.

Once, I did a live video as I was cooking home-made chicken kiev. In the middle of the video, I shared my recipe. I love cooking (and eating great food!) so it is natural for me to talk about it. Again, I received so many comments, mostly along the lines of: *can I have dinner at yours?!*

Storytelling marketing means you get to share all of you. And you stay in the hearts and minds of your audience. Think of all the stories you can tell. Get a pocket-sized notebook and jot them all down — this is valuable material. Factor these moments into your marketing. Make them part of how you put yourself out there. You will hold people's attention for longer and leapfrog the 'know, like and trust' hurdle with ease.

Now let's look at putting a plan around your marketing...

CHAPTER 17: CLEAR MARKETING STRATEGY

Instead of sitting down at the computer and asking yourself *'how will I market today?'*, take the time to plan out the next 6 to 12 months of what you want to offer in your business. This is not a stuffy plan that you create once and shelve. This is dynamic. Unless you have a business that is solid, proven and has worked like clockwork for a number of years, your plan needs to be flexible, but you still need a plan.

In the section above, I talked about the different ways you can package your offer (e.g. a premium package, an online course or a workshop). Ideally, you have a low-priced, mid-priced and a high-end program to suit people at different budgets. Your overall marketing strategy has to be aligned to these offers. If you have an online workshop and a premium package, your focus is on getting people to buy those two products. Your marketing also has to factor in how they find out about you and how they buy the products. Is it through a webinar or workshop? Do they hear about you via word-of-mouth or have you got your website chock full with Google-friendly content?

Reverse engineer your marketing approach to the end result you desire. More about what this looks like shortly.

CONTENT WITH PURPOSE

The biggest challenge I faced when I was coming up with content ideas for my business was creating content for content's sake. It was a way of putting myself out there, but I had no overarching strategy, nor did I put thought into what I wanted the marketing to do for me. Until the moment the lightbulb went off in my head and I realised my content had to have purpose too. You may have grasped this a lot sooner than I did! It dawned on me that unless I had a solid offer or suite of offers, I would not be able to market as effectively as I would like.

This is not to mean I used it as an excuse to stop marketing. 'Unless my marketing is spot on, I won't do any' is a cop out! Business is a series of steps and you are always iterating. This is not a 'get out of jail free' card to stop marketing.

Even though I was unclear, I was still showing up and people were getting to know me, but when you make the connection between what you are selling and what you are marketing, business becomes a lot simpler.

REPURPOSING CONTENT

The key to making your tiny time work for you is to be super smart about what you do in your business and make it work for you over and over again. It's not about creating a video, posting it in a few places and forgetting about it. Re-use that content repeatedly and it will drive traffic to your site and your social media channels over and over.

One way I repurpose content in my business is through my blog. I record one video, upload the video to YouTube, strip the audio for my podcast and get it transcribed as an article. On my blog, you will see video (MP4) and audio (MP3) formats, plus a written blog.

I take one piece of content and repurpose it in three ways to meet the needs of my audience. There are people who love to read, some who prefer to listen, and those who are only interested if they can watch. I meet all three of those needs with one piece of content.

This is leveraging your marketing.

The key to making your tiny time work for you is to be super smart about what you do in your business and make it work for you over and over again.

CHAPTER 18: BUILD, KNOW AND GROW YOUR AUDIENCE

WHAT MARKETING METHODS WILL YOU USE?

Do you need to be online or can you do it all offline? I often hear people say they don't need to be online because they do all their business through networking or referrals. While these are fantastic ways to grow your business, being online means reducing that friction we talked about in the last section. I don't know about you, but as soon as someone mentions a name to me, the first thing I do is visit their website. I read their blog, listen to their podcasts, and watch their videos. I want to get a sense of that person and see if I like their style. I want to know if I resonate with them. If I do, I will sign up for their free gift and will spend some time in their space. Then if they put a compelling offer in front of me, I will be more likely to buy.

When you have tiny time, you need to be mindful of the amount of effort your marketing will take, where your audience is spending time and how to make sure you're in proximity to those potential clients. Your job is to insert yourself into the space where they already spend their time. That's why I recommend a combination of online and offline marketing methods to allow people to resonate with you and reduce friction. Because real people are spending time online and offline.

There are many different ways to market. Every week, you'll hear about the latest 'must-do' marketing strategy! Yes, this can be overwhelming and it can be confusing. As a tiny timer, it is important for you to recognise your limited time availability and know that your success depends on you using the time you have to maximum impact. You'll never hear me say you need to do everything. It's not possible to be everywhere.

Take your marketing back to that science lab. Test and test and test again!

Think about the way you like to communicate, the way your audience likes to communicate, what you are really good at, and then choose your marketing methods based on those criteria. Once you have chosen, be consistent so people know they can trust you. I learnt the value of consistency from my mentors and it is one of the most important factors in your business. If you keep showing up, your clients will show up too.

The reason I recommend marketing both online and offline is to ensure you don't put all your eggs in one basket. Imagine if social media was shut down tomorrow and you'd built your following on one particular channel alone. Your business would be in peril. I don't for one minute think you wouldn't be able to start again because you're that kind of person. But do you really want to?

The key to successful marketing is to find out what works and do more of that! Below I have listed some of the ways you can market. This list is not exhaustive. As you can imagine, the ways to share your message evolve and change constantly, which is why this book is not about how to do these marketing methods. I cover these in greater detail in the Tiny Time Business School.

- Blogging
- Video
- Podcasting
- Speaking
- Networking
- PR
- Email marketing
- Social media — 'broadcasting' and interacting
- Advertising
- Affiliate partners

In my business, my online methods include:

- Email marketing
- Podcast
- YouTube channel
- Blog
- Social media

My offline methods include:

- Speaking
- Networking

My offline methods complement what I do online. Like I've said before, when someone first meets you, their initial instinct will be to check you out online. They will visit your website, will look you up on social media, read your blogs and watch your videos. We all do this! If they like you, they'll want to binge-consume everything you have. Make sure you're ready for them. By this, I mean have at least five blogs and five videos at the ready. You know me, I like to keep it simple!

TINY TIME BIG RESULTS

So now you're marketing your message. People are getting to know you, like you and trust you. How does all this translate into good quality leads?

CHAPTER 19: LEAD GENERATION MADE SIMPLE —THE PINK SPOON STRATEGY

When I was a child, a trip to the cinema was a special occasion. Just the thought of buying sweets and treats was enough to send me giddy for days. I remember the day when I first saw the ice-cream stand and it had 32 flavours. My eyes nearly popped out! I remember thinking: *how on earth am I going to choose?!* The lady behind the counter watched me screw up my face as I looked at the flavours, unable to decide. She then uttered seven magic words: "Would you like to try a bit?" She held out a pink spoon and asked me which one I wanted to try. I still took ages to decide, but that was a defining moment. I could try a bit first.

This is the principle I am going to share with you now. It's called the Pink Spoon Strategy. (Little did I know someone put a name to my ice-cream experience!)

Earlier, I talked about reducing friction in your marketing. The Pink Spoon Strategy creates safety for your prospect. It allows them the opportunity to experience you and your work before buying. Commonly referred to as a lead magnet — because you want leads and need something magnetic to attract them — it also does the job of repelling people you're not interested in having as clients. So for instance, if someone is not interested in attracting and converting clients in 20 hours a week, they won't be interested in my free video series (you can get access here: www.bit.ly/5stepsyv).

If you do not currently offer something free to prospects, you are leaving money on the table because a lead magnet gives people the chance to try your work without making a financial investment, yet gives you the opportunity to start a conversation with them.

When I talk about reverse-engineering your marketing, your lead magnet is a crucial part of this. You need to be clear what you are offering and work backwards. Think of it as your customer journey. They choose your lead magnet, you provide great value and you make an offer. How this looks will be different for each business, but essentially, it's about a series of small 'yeses'. A sequence of micro-commitments that your prospect makes.

As with everything in marketing, it's all about creating safety and reducing friction.

HOW DO YOU CHOOSE THE TOPIC OF YOUR LEAD MAGNET?

Think back to the transformation you offer, the end result you help people create. Take one piece out of the process and package this as your lead magnet, so you audience gets a taster. Their next step would be to buy your package, program or service.

For example, when I launched Tiny Time Business School for the first time, I created a series of free online trainings that covered specific topics in one particular module. I delivered online training on how to write a newsletter that brings in paying clients, how to do sales conversations that convert and how to attract clients using webinars.

You can offer a free cheat-sheet, challenge, or PDF guide, an eBook, a quiz, an assessment or a report as your lead magnet. The options are endless. When you're creating your lead magnet, you want to make it easy to consume and highly valuable. We go into more depth on how to do this in the Tiny Time Business School (www.yasminvorajee.com/tinytimebusinessschool)

As well as a lead magnet for specific products, you may want one for your business or website as a whole. To entice new leads 24/7, I have a free video series on how to attract and convert clients in less than 20 hours a week. I also have a free cheat-sheet on the 20 tools I use to help me work smarter, not harder and a free cheatsheet on how to turn one program into multiple streams of income. You can access these in the Book Club (www.yasminvorajee.com/jointtbookclub). I promote these wherever I can to ensure I am attracting new leads all the time.

When someone wants to find out more about me, I want them to experience me for free, get a sense of my style and resonate with me. Your lead magnet will give people the chance to do this and make it safe for them to do so.

Once you have created your lead magnet, you will need a webpage for them to provide their details so you can send it to them.

Short-term Nurturing

Once someone opts in for your free gift, you begin a conversation with your prospect to move them towards a buying decision. To do this, you need to nurture them.

There are two types of nurture — short-term and long-term. Think of it as meeting someone for the first time. When you meet someone, you might have coffee together and you're a little smitten. If they then disappeared from your life and showed up six months later when they needed a date for their cousin's wedding, how likely would you be to say, "Yes, I'd love to go!"? Not very likely! There is no rapport between you. That person has not nurtured you or the relationship.

It's exactly the same in business. How many times have you signed up for a free gift, only to have them disappear and then pop back into your inbox when they have something to sell?

You don't want to be that person. Once someone has opted in to get your lead magnet, you want to create a nurturing sequence of events for the next 7-10 days. Schedule a message every other day so it's not a case of overkill.

If we continue the dating analogy, this part is like when you're messaging each other. Your short-term nurture sequence could include a series of emails to help them implement aspects of your free gift, give them examples of how your product or service could help them, and a chance for them to get to know you and your personality. It could be a series of short bite-sized videos.

Especially for you as a tiny timer, it's key that this is automated using an email autoresponder, so it works like clockwork once you've set it up!

Your objective for the short-term nurturing is to give them more reasons to fall in love with you. You want to elicit a specific response in people, which is why it's so important to be strong with your marketing message, what you stand for and what you believe in. When you do that, you will magnetise your people and repel everybody else. And that is exactly the reaction you want.

In some of my videos, I have my baby with me. Sometimes, he decides that is the moment he wants a feed so he will start hitting my chest. (That's his cue!) I have often started to breastfeed during a live video (not that you can see anything, because I'm very discreet, but you'll know I am feeding). Some people don't like this and I am okay with that! Others love it. It's who I am. And I'm happy that it either attracts or repels people.

The aim of the short-term sequence is to create rapport and resonance with your prospects.

Long-term Nurturing

The short-term sequence is for the first one or two weeks of 'meeting you'. At that stage, you then take a step back so you don't annoy or exhaust the new lead. They need room to breathe too!

At this point, switch from an intense nurturing position to a low-key-but-present strategy by showing up in their inbox every week or month. You decide the frequency based on what you know about your audience and your time. Once you have decided the frequency, then aim to be consistent to show you can be trusted. Trust is key, which is why I advise starting off with something manageable like once a month if you're worried that you can't commit to more. A weekly or monthly newsletter is a great way to stay in front of your prospects, be front-of-mind, and continue the rapport and relationship-building.

People will buy when they are ready to buy, not when you are ready to sell. If you have been consistent with communicating with them, they are more likely to do business with you than with someone they have never 'met' before.

If you struggle with what to include in your newsletter, you don't need to create fresh content every time. Use it as a way to share your blog, your podcast or any videos you may have done that week. Don't just keep showing up in their inbox with no offers. You have an engaged audience now. You've put effort into nurturing them. Make sure you are sharing what you sell. Give your prospect clear calls to action, invite them to book a consultation, use a voucher for their next purchase or attend your online workshop.

In the same way your content has a purpose, your long-term nurturing sequence also has a purpose. You are growing the 'know, like, trust' factor. You are giving value. And you are letting them know what you have to sell. Some business owners are great at the first two, but are afraid of the third one — selling their stuff — because they don't want to come across as salesy. We'll cover this shortly, but all you need to know for now is this: I have clients who followed me for years before they were ready to buy. I also have clients who decided to work with me within one week of receiving my lead magnet. People buy when they're ready to buy, not when you're ready to sell. I can't emphasise that enough! And that is why nurturing is so crucial.

MANUAL AND AUTOMATED LEAD GENERATION

Your business will always need a flood of leads to ensure your profitability and sustainability, so think about how you can continue to drive traffic to your lead magnet. I would recommend using every bit of online and offline space you have to keep the gift in front of people.

Put your lead magnet on your website, your social media channels, at the end of every video or blog, on every podcast episode, on every photo, at speaking engagements or on your business card. You may have a number of opt-in gifts so decide where it makes sense for them to be.

Use paid advertising to drive traffic to your lead magnets, and always make sure you send people to your lead magnet first and not your sales pages, as you want to warm up your leads first.

In the spirit of keeping things simple, remember to start with one. You will grow your business infrastructure like lead magnets and nurturing sequences one by one. You don't build a house in one fell swoop — you do it brick by brick.

Now let's turn those leads into sales!

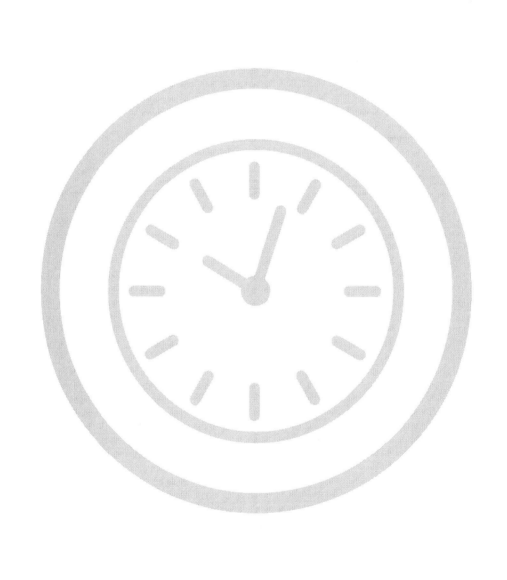

PROFIT PRINCIPLE PART 4: CLIENT CONVERSION

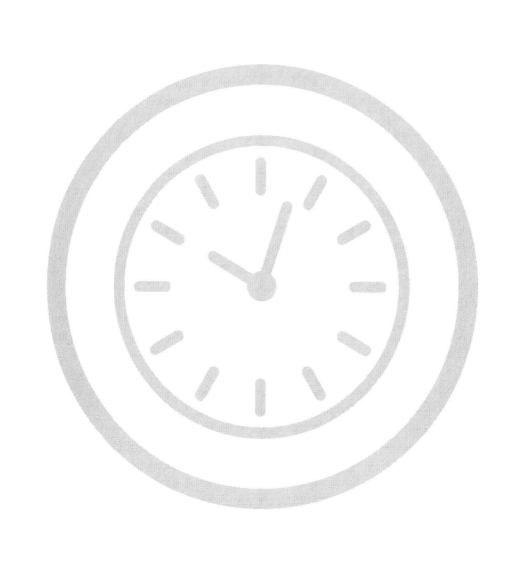

CHAPTER 20: TURNING LEADS INTO SALES

Converting prospects into paying clients is the piece many people overlook or struggle with. I did too. But unless you master your conversion process, you will have lots of leads but no money coming in. Until money changes hands, nothing happens so you need to get really good at this. (Sorry for breaking the bad news, but if you do hate sales and selling, this part will turn that ship around!)

Before we get into the nuts and bolts of selling the tiny-time way, I want to help you shift your mindset around sales and selling, and fall in love with what sales does for you and your prospect.

FALL IN LOVE WITH SALES

Shortly after I started my business, I was out for dinner with colleagues and the conversation turned to sales. One of my colleagues said she was not a sales person, and when she spoke about sales and selling, her voice dripped with disdain. She didn't regard herself as a sales person. And for good reason.

When we were younger, my dad used to take us to car showrooms all the time. (He still does this with his grandchildren!) As we walked around, car salesmen would approach him and after listening to them for a few minutes, I was turned off with their sales spiel.

A sales spiel puts pressure on you to buy something you don't need or want. It is frequently accompanied by an icky feeling when the sales person taps into your insecurities to make the sale at all costs. This approach smacks of sneaky manipulation and using NLP techniques on people to make them buy what they don't need. If you've had similar experiences, the last thing you want is to be likened to those people. It's no wonder some of us don't want to identify with the label of sales.

At the start of my corporate career, I worked in a call centre where selling was considered the most important function of the staff in all departments. Even when the customer didn't want it! The leads on the other end of the line were normally faced with a shopping list of offers made one after another. This was uncomfortable for the customer and for the sales person, but the sales person knew they had to do it, otherwise they would be penalised, their monthly incentive payments would suffer and it would damage their promotion prospects.

When it comes to your own business, though, you know you have something **valuable** to offer. You act with integrity and make offers based on what you think your customer wants. It is up to them to say yes or no. You don't get attached to the outcome... (Easy to say. Hard but essential to do!)

I was one of those people who prided themselves on not selling. As far as I concerned, it was sleazy. Until I started my business and realised... if I didn't sell, I didn't make money. It's so simple yet how many of us resist the idea of selling? When I heard the phrase 'to sell is to serve' in my corporate days, I would shudder. Selling was forced down people's throats whether they wanted it or not. But to sell *is* to serve in your case. If you have an amazing service and you don't let anybody know about it, you are doing them a disservice. You're not able to serve because you are refusing to sell. And that is the biggest difference when it comes to selling something you believe in and something you don't believe in.

Here are five ways to shift your mindset and fall in love with selling:

1: Fall in love with what brings in the money

In business, you have to be making offers, not just offering free stuff! Free is great for people to get a taster of what you do, but you don't want your audience to get used to everything being free. They don't appreciate when you start to charge — so charge from the beginning! It's a trap I've seen a lot of people fall into. If you're in business, you need to sell. Please don't get caught up in the illusion that you're selling by offering lots of free content. Until you make an offer, you're not selling!

Recently, one of my clients asked me about the number of offers I make on a regular and consistent basis. She wanted to know how I could make so many offers and how I delivered on them. The reason I make offers is to have consistent cash-flow. I create those offers to test what my audience wants, so people see what I have to sell. And I put them out regularly so my audience knows I do sell and don't just put out free content. Don't get me wrong. I put out a lot of free content in the form of videos, podcast episodes, how-to guides, five-day challenges and free eBooks. But I'm also in the business of being in business. Selling is how I keep that machine going. I do it in a way that feels good to me, aligns with my values and serves at a higher level.

2: Fall in love with the person you're here to serve

When you get to know the people you're here to serve and you have a deep desire to serve them, selling becomes so much easier. There are no anxieties about offering to these people because you have something that makes their life so much better. Whether that's by offering them beautiful wedding pictures or helping them lose 5lbs. By not selling, you're depriving them of the opportunity to get what they really want out of life. And you don't want to do that, do you?

3: Fall deeply and madly in love with your offer

If you know that your product, service or program really helps people and you believe in it wholeheartedly, this will shine through for you. When you're talking to prospects, your enthusiasm and excitement will be undeniable. Focus and hone that absolute love of what you do when talking to prospects.

In my corporate career in a call centre environment, this was something we talked a lot about in our training modules and workshops. When talking to prospects, the emphasis is not about the features of your product but about what it can do for them. I have to admit, in the corporate environment, I didn't really feel it. In my own business, though? Absolutely! I know exactly what my programs, services and products can do for you. I believe in them.

The question you need to ask yourself is: *do I love what I offer?* If the answer is yes, go forth and share that! If not, what could you do to make your offers epic?

4: Fall in love with the value

The one area that most people struggle with when it comes to having a great sales conversation (me included!) is knowing how to articulate the value of your offer. Your job is to identify what it would mean to the other person if they got value from working with you.

Whether it's learning how to speak with greater authority in meetings, creating a powerful executive presence, getting their toddler to sleep through the night, creating simple healthy meals or knowing how to date online, you are making a difference. Always talk about the value of that difference you make. Selling beautiful lingerie? Same principle applies. Selling exercise or eating plans? Same principle applies.

Step into your power and articulate the value as if you're selling to yourself. You have to be able to sell it to yourself before you can sell to anyone else. Create at least 10 reasons your product, service or program makes that person's life better.

If you can't articulate the value, you will be hit with all the usual objections and not know how to answer them.

- 'It's too expensive!' (Compared to what?)

- 'I can't afford it.' (You can't afford not to when it comes to what it will do for you.)

- 'I haven't got the time.' (Think of all the time you'll save by doing this.)

When describing the value of your offer, here are two powerful little words you can use.

"So that...."

I want you to paint a picture for your prospect. Look at your list of 10 reasons and add those two words before each one. Here's an example:

Using my unique formula, you'll be able to get your toddler to sleep through...

- **So that** *you can enjoy some quiet time with your partner.*

- **So that** *you can get a chapter of your book written.*

- **So that** *you can get the packed lunches ready and still watch your favourite TV show.*

- **So that** *you can read your book.*

- **So that** *you can take a bath.*

As a mum of three, getting 'me time' is high on my list of priorities, so anything that makes me think I can have two or three hours to myself will always win!

Painting a picture means you invoke emotions. And it's emotion not logic that makes the sale happen. People buy on emotion, and as long as you have their best interests at heart, you will be able to help far more people. Once you fall in love with the value of your offer, share it!

5: Be fearless when it comes to the money conversation

Be prepared, this is a big one. Many sales have gone by the wayside because people are not willing to have the money conversation. When you refuse to talk about why someone thinks you're too expensive, or if they say they can't afford it or they don't have the time <insert all the other objections you get here>, you leave money on the table.

Being fearless with the money conversation doesn't mean you get bolshie or aggressive. Being fearless means you tackle the topic. You aim isn't to make them feel bad for not being able to afford you or needing to talk to their husband/wife/partner, but when the objection arises, you face it head on. Instead of slinking away and saying, "Okay, maybe next time".

Have you ever had someone tell you they can't afford your package, then the following week, you see them sharing all over Facebook how they've signed up for <insert crazy expensive course> that costs way more than what you were offering? You spend the rest of the afternoon wondering why they said they couldn't afford you!

That common scenario happens when you prime someone for a sale during your sales conversation, then when you're fearful of the money talk, you let them slip through. The point is **they're still looking for a solution**. When someone else comes along offering a solution and is able to articulate the value, they sign right up! All your hard work has now benefitted someone else! If you don't want this to happen, don't be afraid of the money conversation!

KNOW YOUR NUMBERS

Sales is a numbers game so understanding your numbers is crucial to your success. It's not about having fancy spreadsheets, full of pivot tables or macros. (I don't even know what those are — I just use a simple Excel sheet.) However, it is important to track all the sales conversations you have booked in, the ones you have completed and the outcomes. This allows you to track your conversion rate and identify what you need to work on to improve it.

Knowing your numbers means you can also plan your time better. If you want to sign two new clients per month and you currently have a 20% conversion rate, you will need 10 appointments booked in with a margin of two extra in case of no-shows. If your conversion rate is higher, the number of appointments you need will be lower. But you won't know this if you don't track!

Improving your conversion rate is a series of small actions before, during and after the sales conversation.

Let's talk about those now.

GET APPOINTMENT-READY

How do you currently set appointments? Do you invite people to email you or call you to set up a time? Getting appointment-ready is a simple action you can take that will save you hundreds of hours over the lifetime of your business.

Instead of emailing back and forth about suitable dates and times, get savvy with your time and technology and use an online calendar where you set the times you are available for appointments. Then share this link with your prospects so they can choose the time that suits them. It's all automated and fuss-free. I love using this approach because you can also ask questions prior to the appointment to determine if they are a good fit for you.

I invited a client of mine to implement this for dress-fitting appointments in her business. She was that soldier, emailing back and forth, constantly trying to find suitable times. She was exhausted from it! It was sucking up so much of her time unnecessarily. It took less than an hour to get the appointments system set up with a questionnaire. In one fell swoop, she automated this time-wasting activity and gave herself back the gift of hours and sanity.

Getting appointment-ready is the first step. The next step is to pre-sell.

Pre-Sell Your Prospect

When someone books in for an appointment, use this as an opportunity to wow them *before* they get on a call with you. You can share your most popular blogs with them, a free training or client testimonials. The objective is to get them excited about working with you before the call. In effect, you're pre-selling them.

This can be easily automated so you set it up once and it works for you again and again!

Now let's move on to the sales conversation.

THE SALES CONVERSATION

Do you get nervous before a sales conversation? Do you find it hard to concentrate on anything else? Do you get wound up thinking they have to say yes? I have done all of the above so you're in good company. The problem is getting nervous, wound up or overly attached to the outcome doesn't help you to have a great sales conversation.

When someone has a sales call with me, I want it to be a good experience for them. Even if they decide to not work with me, I want them to walk away thinking *that was a useful and valuable call*. They may not buy right now, but when the time is right, they will come back. Only, though, if they have a good experience.

The purpose of the sales conversation is to establish a gap. A gap between where your prospect is right now and where they want to be. Your job is to get your prospect and yourself very clear on this gap. (Be sure to ask lots of questions!) You have to help them articulate the gap, understand the cost of it to them (in their life, their relationships, their health, their work and so on), and determine how urgent their need is to resolve it. If you ask someone how urgent their need is on a scale of 1-10 (with 1 being not urgent at all), and their reply is anything less than a 7, you need to walk away. They don't feel the discomfort of the situation enough to make an investment in resolving it.

This goes back to the work you did earlier on understanding your target audience. You want your ideal client to be hungry for what you do. I have often spoken to people who say 'I'm thinking about doing this'. However I get the sense that this is something they're only just beginning to consider and are not ready to take action, I will advise them to get back in touch when they are ready. There is nothing more frustrating than working with somebody who is not committed to the end result. You do your bit but your client has to take action too. You don't want a situation where your client doesn't act and you take the blame for it!

Take time to establish the gap and avoid premature presentation! That is: don't be too quick to make your offer when you haven't taken enough time to truly understand the challenge and how you can help them. If you have not established the gap sufficiently and you make an offer, you may be jumping the gun. This isn't always the case. When you have tweaked your process and are now getting qualified prospects coming into your sales appointments, it will be easier. Like anything worthwhile, this takes time!

The sales conversation is a series of steps, starting from building a rapport, setting expectations about what the call is about (where you take the lead and let them know how the call will go), and then asking about their current reality. The sales conversation is not a chat; it's a structured conversation.

Once you've established where they are, then ask them where they want to be. Get them excited about what it could look like. I would avoid asking questions that are too far into the future, as that can feel unreal for your prospect. Instead ask them what they want to achieve in the next 6 to 12 months. Connect them to their big vision then help to break that down into the next 6 to 12 months so it feels more do-able and real.

I recommend only presenting your offer when the prospect asks you for the information. Until they ask, there is not enough tension built. If you start talking about the offer too quickly, they may not be ready for it. Once the prospective client has asked about the offer, please do not fall into the trap of talking about the *how* of your offer. If you were planning a holiday, you would not be excited if the travel agent kept talking about how gorgeous the plane was, how soft the seats would be and how many miles an hour the plane travelled. You don't care about that. You want to know what the weather is like at your destination. You want to know about the hotel, the food and how you are going to feel once you are on holiday. You want the consultant to show you pictures of the sun loungers and the beach area. Your prospect is exactly the same.

In the sales conversation, focus on the destination, not the journey. Talk about the end result your offer will help them create. Present the price when they ask how much is it. Tell them about the logistics of the offer, but don't make it all about the features. Keep talking about the benefits.

A powerful way to connect with your prospect is to make a note of the words they use when they describe their problem and their desired reality. If you can use their words when you're presenting your offer, it will show them you have listened, and connected with where they are and where they want to be. They will trust you more because they feel you understand them fully. Aim to cover their potential objections (too pricey, don't have the time etc.) before you present the offer.

This is about connection and building rapport, not about manipulating your prospects. When you present your price, always talk about the value you are offering. In the sales conversation, you want to convey the value as much as you can, so by the time you present the price, it's a done deal!

Those are the sweetest moments: when you present a price, they respond positively and are ready to pay you there and then!

Decision Time

When you have made your offer, if your prospect is happy to proceed, take payment or make arrangements for how payment will be made. Take a deposit so they are committed. Don't let them go away with no arrangement for payment. Let them know you'll send them an invoice or take their payment while you're still on the call.

If your prospect is hesitating, probe deeper into why they are hesitating. This is not something to be afraid of. Your prospect is a real human being with fears and concerns. Your job is to stand in a position of leadership and show them you can help them. You want to connect your humanity to their humanity. But if someone is having a wobble, don't wobble with them.

They need your belief in them to be greater than their doubts.

Give them space to think about it. I don't believe in pushing for a decision immediately. I will empower my prospect with what they need to make a decision and arrange to follow up. Some sales experts will say my approach means I leave money on the table, but I am comfortable with my approach, because nine times out of ten, that prospect comes back and I make the sale. If I had pushed for a sale that they weren't ready to make, I am doing them a disservice.

When you are clear on who you want to work with and their attributes, you will know if your prospect is a good fit. Then it's just about making sure this conversion happens. The key to successful sales conversations is practice and lots of it! Role-playing sales conversations is a brilliant way to grow your confidence, but it will be an ongoing work in progress! I'm still learning, refining and honing my sales process. That is normal.

Of course, sometimes you won't get an immediate yes, even if you follow the lead generation and sales conversation advice to the letter. Here's what to do next.

AFTER THE SALES CONVERSATION

Ask the prospect how much time they need to think about the offer and schedule in a follow-up. Specify a date and time, and put it in your diary. It is imperative you don't leave it hanging in mid-air with a vague 'let's catch up next week' statement. Make a date in your diary and schedule it in.

To aid the decision-making process, I recommend creating a document that summarises what you have discussed and what you are proposing. This is useful to help both parties be clear in their minds about the offer on the table. It's also a great opportunity for you to re-state the value.

I wouldn't leave it more than a week in between the sales call and the follow-up session. (If holidays or other commitments prevent that, it's unfortunate, but there's only so much you can do.) If you have done a great job on the sales call of building the tension (just like blowing up a balloon), then you don't want to allow too much time for them to lose excitement and anticipation about achieving their outcome (the balloon deflating).

You also don't want to create too much space for the monkey mind… Let's address that now.

TAMING THE MONKEY MIND

Your monkey mind wants to keep you safe no matter what. Your brain will do whatever it takes to keep you safe, even if it's in a situation you don't particularly like. If you're safe there, your monkey mind likes that and aims to keep you there. When you have this awareness, you can work around it. Your prospect is exactly the same. Their monkey mind is trying to keep them safe at all costs... And you may be seen as the threat. This is why you have to show up in the sales conversation as a leader. You need to stand up for your potential client and show them what is possible.

It's all too easy to get frustrated if you've had sales call after sales call and each time it's been a no. That happens to me too. I understand how you start questioning everything. It's easy to go down a rabbit hole of 'nobody wants me', 'I'm too expensive' or 'this business will never work', but thinking like that is unproductive.

Instead, use this time to reset your satellite navigation! Establish your ideal client. Get clear and focused on who you want to work with, then send an intention out into the Universe that you want to magnetise that ideal client to you. Magnetise people who love what you do, can afford you, are willing to pay and behave like they're keen.

Don't let your monkey mind run the show. Your monkey mind is simply your fear and nothing good ever comes from letting your fear run amok. Liz Gilbert says it beautifully in her book *Big Magic*: "Fear is part of you. It can have a seat in the bus of you, but it is **forbidden** to drive!"

FOLLOW UP

Following up is the one thing you can do that will put you far ahead of the competition, simply because a lot of people won't do it! They believe it's icky and feel resistant to doing it.

Perhaps when you had a sales conversation and followed up a month ago, it was a 'no' or 'not right now'. Don't just leave it there. The majority of business is won in the follow up so this is where you have to put your fear (about people thinking you're pushy or salesy) to one side. Make a note to drop them a quick message and check in to see how they are.

If they're on your mailing list, they will continue to be nurtured through your regular newsletter, but you also want to maintain a regular connection with them, so that you will be their first port of call when they are ready to buy.

When you're tracking your sales conversations, make a note of when you plan to follow up with people. And stick to it! Most business owners don't follow up ever. If you do, you'll be in a tiny minority, and you and your business will thrive as a result.

STICKY SALES

Once somebody has paid, you want to reinforce that they have made a great decision and magnify their excitement! You could send them a quick video congratulating them on their decision. It could be a gift of a relevant book or an assignment that they can get started with immediately.

ONE LAST WORD ON SALES

Don't **ever** be afraid of sharing your message with people. If someone is not interested, most people are perfectly capable of saying a polite 'no thank you'. If you've made an offer and it doesn't suit them, they can simply say 'it's not for me'.

There will be people from time to time who will react badly when you make an offer. Here's my word of advice... **don't let them stop you!** In 99% of the cases, their response is about them. Maybe they're in business too and hate the idea of selling, so when you make an offer, you trigger something in them. It doesn't really matter why. What matters is that you **never** — never, never, never — let someone take away your power and stop you from selling.

When you make offers and people are excited to work with you, hold that image in your mind. There are more of those people than the ones who react badly, so focus your energies on them **only**.

I would never have joined a mastermind group if the coach leading it had not reached out to me and asked me if I was interested in having a chat. Back then, I was not in the market for a mastermind. But when Sarah approached me, I was open to the conversation. I signed up for the mastermind and had an amazing nine months with a wonderful group of women who to this day are great friends of mine and have seen me through highs and lows. None of that would have happened if I had not been approached.

If you were to stop offering your products, programs and services simply because a handful (and there's never more than that) took offence that you dared to make an offer, think about all the people who would miss out on you. On the transformation you create for them. On the positive difference you make to people's lives. All because someone got triggered by you making an offer and selling to them.

It's not about you. It's truly about them. Stay on the path, keep offering and you will thrive. You will be surrounded by the people who love you and value your work. I speak from the heart on this because it happened to me and it could have derailed me. I'll admit I have thin skin. I take everything to heart. It feels like a punch in the stomach. I feel winded and wounded. But we are bigger than that! We're here for a more powerful purpose and it's times like this you realise your own power. Step into it and know you're here to serve. Yes, sometimes that gets messy. But most of the time, **it is glorious.** So never stop selling, never stop offering and never let anyone dull your shine!

That's me off my soapbox; now let's talk about turning your new client into a raving fan!

*Don't **ever** be afraid of sharing your message with people. If someone is not interested, most people are perfectly capable of saying a polite 'no thank you'. If you've made an offer and it doesn't suit them, they can simply say 'it's not for me'.*

CHAPTER 21: CLIENT DELIGHT

You have a new client! What happens next? So much effort is placed on client attraction that you may be forgiven for thinking your work is done once they sign up. However, winning the client is only half the job. Now you have to deliver on your promise (which we covered in Part 2: Leverage)!

In addition to a solid program or service delivery, here are three simple strategies you can implement to help you delight your client and set expectations.

ON-BOARDING

When you welcome a new client, let them know how you'll work together, what to expect from you, how to get in touch and how to resolve any issues. Clarity from the beginning is crucial to ensure a healthy working relationship.

When I was in corporate, one of my responsibilities when I was VP of Leadership Development was executive on-boarding. This process was to ensure a smooth transition into the role and ironing out any issues or challenges.

In your business, you determine what this looks like for your client and you create an on-boarding process. It can be as simple as a welcome pack. (By now, you know how much I like to keep things as simple as possible!)

Once you have this process working well, you can outsource when appropriate.

PROTECT YOURSELF AND YOUR CLIENT

When you start working with someone, it's important to be clear on your expectations of each other. It's equally important to make sure you have terms and conditions attached to working with you. This gives you the confidence and protection you need should any problems arise, such as late payments or grievances about the work.

When a new client starts working with you, set your terms and conditions and include them as part of your on-boarding. This will give you peace of mind, in case anything does go awry. Life happens. You can't avoid that. But you can protect yourself and your business. We talk more about how to do this in the Tiny Time Business School www.yasminvorajee.com/tinytimebusinessschool

CLIENT EXPERIENCE

When a client works with you, you want them to have a great experience. I would encourage you to keep this front of mind all the time. This does not mean you bend over backwards for your clients, but your aim is not to just have this client for a one-time sale. You want to create raving fans who will do the best marketing your business will ever have — word of mouth. People buy from people. So if your clients love working with you, they will refer you to others. (Unless, of course, they want to keep you all to themselves!)

Your aim is for your client to be happy working with you. Think about how you communicate, the look and feel of what working with you is like.

For example, when I hold in-person VIP days, I run them in lovely nurturing environments. I make sure the materials I create are high quality. I use some secret strategies to delight my clients too, which I don't publicise because I don't want it to become something people expect instead of a lovely surprise! I would recommend the same for you — keep a few wonderful treats up your sleeve to surprise and delight!

THE PROFIT PRINCIPLE IN A NUTSHELL

Making your business profitable in tiny time is about a series of steps you take to ensure you attract a flood of leads that translate into sales and happy clients who rave about you.

To run a profitable business in 20 hours a week, being profitable means you

- Have leveraged products and services where you sell value, not time
- Know your numbers!
- Keep your costs low
- Have a strategic and deliberate client attraction strategy
- Have a proven client attraction strategy that works to your strengths in the time you have
- Create a solid and effective client conversion strategy
- Aim to create raving fans for life!

Now let's talk about how to amplify your time!

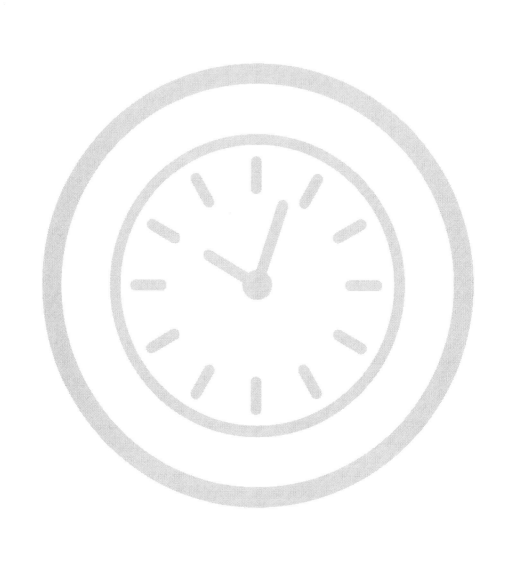

SECTION 5: THE PRODUCTIVITY PRINCIPLE

Productivity is being able to do things that you were never able to do before.

— Franz Kafka

The Profit Principle is chunky, but once you have the business model sorted out, you have to structure your business to make sure you squeeze every bit of juice from the time you work. If you sit down to work for three hours and you are easily distracted with social media, the internet or your emails, which you trawl through instead of doing the work that brings you a return, your tiny time will always be your biggest trial.

This is when the simple strategies and ideas I share here will help you get focused and work on what brings you a result. Get ready to trim the fat!

CHAPTER 22: TINY TIME IS THE OPPORTUNITY

The 80/20 rule states that for many events, roughly 80% of the effects come from 20% of the causes. Otherwise known as Pareto's Rule, this means 80% of your results in business can be attributed to 20% of your activities. You generate 80% of your revenue from 20% of your clients. You wear 20% of your clothes 80% of the time.

I had heard about the 80/20 principle many times before, but it was only once I started down the tiny time journey that I realised how relevant it was to my own approach and how beautifully it applied to the tiny-time world.

As I mentioned in the Profit Principle, premium packages are one of my favourite ways to generate revenues. I don't need many of those clients to have a healthy income and creating digital assets means you create once, sell repeatedly.

It is critical to get the most out of your time, and doing so requires a level of focus and concentration. For example, right now, my eldest is on school holidays. He and the baby are engrossed in *The Lego Batman Movie*. I am writing this as they watch and am keenly aware of the limited pocket of time available to me. Needless to say, I am not looking at emails or social media!

Often business owners will complain about a lack of time and believe this is their biggest challenge. I believe our words have great power, so instead of thinking that lack of time is a challenge, I prefer to see it as a unique opportunity. An opportunity to see what is possible when you have a limited resource and how resourceful you can become.

In this section, I will be sharing strategies and ideas on how you can be more productive with your time. The profit section laid the foundations of a sustainable business that allows you to attract and convert clients consistently, as well as how to scale your business through the power of leverage. When you have a solid foundation like that, you become more productive because you're focused on the work that creates a result. The work that makes a difference, drives revenue, grows your business and creates an impact for the people you're here to serve.

If you're a busy business owner and you're working on the wrong things, you have your ladder against the wrong wall. No amount of work will compensate for a faulty foundation. As you're reading through this Productivity Principle, know that you don't have to do all of these. Tiny time is about working smarter, not harder! Whereas the Profit Principle was about simplifying your business model and amplifying how you attract and convert clients, the Productivity Principle is all about amplifying your tiny time!

CHAPTER 23: HOW I WORK

Before we dive into the strategies, I want to share how I organise my work week. Despite the messaging I present for my clients, I myself don't work 20 hours a week. For me, it's more like 15 hours. I allocate my work hours across Monday to Friday, from 9am to 12 midday when the children are in school.

I aim to get the bulk of the day's work done between the hours of 9 and 12. I may do an hour later if I get the chance. I try not to work during school holidays, simply because the stress of trying to keep the children occupied keeps me busy enough! Sometimes, I will wake extra early and get work done before the rest of the house is up, but normally, I like to keep that time for my meditation, yoga and journaling so I'm set up for the day. I'll talk more about your morning routine in the Play Principle coming up next.

I also have mornings when it's hard to drag myself out of bed because I stayed up too late the night before to get some 'me time' or 'us time' after the kids had gone to sleep. My daughter started school recently and the baby has just started in crèche, which has freed up more time. As they get older, our schedules will change, I will have a second job as Taxi of Mum, and my business working time will flex to suit the changing needs of my family.

The key part for me is to have an adaptable business and not to be afraid to call in for reinforcements when needed!

I am cognisant of not stuffing my day with more things to do as the kids get busier with school and activities. I love what I do and would love to do more of it, but not at the expense of my time. That's why all my offerings are highly leveraged.

I may decide to only work three or four days a week in future and take up new hobbies. Knowing your business works in teeny tiny pockets of time — as I do now — means you can make it work in that same 20 hours, even if you have the gift of more time.

This is the beauty of making a business work in tiny time. It is a unique opportunity to decide how to work and live!

I may decide to only work three or four days a week in future and take up new hobbies. Knowing your business works in teeny tiny pockets of time — as I do now — means you can make it work in that same 20 hours, even if you have the gift of more time.

CHAPTER 24: STRATEGIES

Declutter First! Before we start to amplify your tiny time, declutter your surroundings. And this doesn't just mean moving things around.

I like to work on a neat and tidy desk, but more often than not, my desk is full of paper, old coffee cups, kids' drawings and lots of tissues! But a cluttered desk doesn't help me to do my best work. It gives me a headache and makes me feel overwhelmed.

That's why your first port of call is to declutter your surroundings, so you can free yourself, your ideas and your creativity. Clutter is a reflection of stagnant energy. When you clear it, you not only clear the environment but your energy too. The fastest way to clear up the energy around your business is to clear the physical space around you, starting with **your desk space.**

I'm not asking you to clear your drawers or anything too taxing but if you're trying to work under a mound of paper and Post-Its, chances are your head's a bit full!

With that in mind, take 10 minutes to clear the top of your desk (or work space) so you can see your desk again. Create an 'IN' pile and an 'OUT' pile. Decluttering is powerful and you don't have to restrict yourself to your work space. If you work from home like I do, tackle one room at a time and do a deep declutter on a regular basis.

90-DAY SPRINTS

When I started my business, I remember creating this lovely business plan. I put time and effort into it and I filed it away... never to look at it again! Can you relate?

When you first start out in business, the focus is on bringing the money in. Without money coming in, your business will gasp for air. But the problem is always chasing the money will lead to damaging short-term thinking.

"If I can just make enough to cover next month's bills, I'll be doing okay."

Then you realise you've been doing that every month and your long-term plans are still sitting on the side-lines.

If you stay in this frame of mind and live month to month, you'll discover quickly it's not sustainable. You'll be exhausted and you'll want to give up. However, if you plan out what you're going to do, you're far more likely to stay on course than without a plan. Failing to plan is planning to fail, after all.

Having said that, I find the annual planning process hard to do! I have a short attention span and planning for a full 12 months feels too abstract for me.

"How can I plan for November when I don't even know what July or even January will look like?"

Instead, I like to break my planning down into chunks of 12 weeks or 90 days. This means that instead of planning for 12 months and feeling disappointed if the first six months haven't gone to plan then deluding myself that I can make up the shortfall in the following six months, I'm more focused on what I am achieving in the next quarter. Working in 90-day blocks means I won't take my eye off the ball by assuming I can make up shortfalls later. If I am not constantly course-correcting, there is something going wrong with my planning process!

This means creating a plan for the next 90 days and working on that and that **alone**.

Think of marketing as planting seeds. You need to give the seeds at least three months to bear fruit. You may not be happy with your results right now, but that's okay. It takes time to build momentum. If you want clients in six months' time, you need to be marketing now. If you don't have clients now, you weren't marketing consistently six months ago.

You will get there, but only if you have a robust plan for the 12 weeks. That means building in your marketing, knowing what you're offering and factoring in your downtime. There is no need to have your nose to the grindstone. You have to know what you're focused on every day and week to achieve the results you want. This approach will prevent you from sitting at your desk wondering what to work on. You will already know.

Once you have planned for the next 90 days, you need to break it down into months and weeks, which means getting clear on your deliverables. This allows you time to breathe and plan instead of leaving everything to the last minute. Once you have broken down your plan into months and weeks, then look at how you organise your days.

One of my biggest challenges (especially with little ones) is not letting my day run away on me. Which is why I have specific working hours and use this time to get the important work done. When you have a clear idea of your top three outcomes for the week, break each deliverable down into specific actions and allocate a day to do them or spread them between your working hours. Every business will be different so it's about making it work for you.

This method of planning will help you know what to focus on and help you get a good night's sleep, because with a plan, you're not keeping your to-do list in your head!

STANDARD OPERATING PROCEDURES

For every job you do in your business, aim to create a process around it so you know what needs to happen and by when. This is commonly referred to as your standard operating procedures (SOPs). SOPs make it much easier for you to complete tasks because you have a process for it.

It's simple to do. Take a blank piece of paper or open a new Word document. List out all the steps you take to complete a particular process. I find it easier to do this when I am actually doing the task — when you do this from memory, you often miss small details. Assign details of deadlines where applicable and who is responsible. That's all you have to do.

You might think you don't need standard operating procedures because it is only you in the business. However, this is short-term thinking, because as your business grows, you will come to a point when you need to outsource or delegate key tasks. If you have SOPs outlined, this will make delegating much easier and less stressful.

BATCH YOUR WORK

One way to make life easier for yourself is to create your content (e.g. blogs, videos, podcasts, press releases etc.) in batches. I recommend this approach because it can be hard to switch from one type of task to another. You need a particular energy to do creative work. When you're creating, you're inviting ideas to pour into you. I believe that ideas are a way of talking to Divine Intelligence — what some call the Source or God or <insert your belief here> — but when I start to do something like filing, I stop that flow. And it's hard to get back in the flow again.

So instead of trying to do a little bit of content creation every day (like your video or blog post, for example), try batching any creative tasks. You can apply the same principle to your paperwork. Do it in one batch. If you're scheduling your social media posts, do them in a batch.

Which leads me nicely to the next strategy...

USE PARKINSON'S LAW TO YOUR ADVANTAGE

This is a law that will change your life, because it gets you focused like never before. Parkinson's Law states that: *work expands to fill the time available for its completion*. If you tell yourself you have all day to do one blog post, it will take you all day! If you give yourself three hours to shoot one two-minute video, it will take you three hours.

The time you allocate to the task will be filled. So I want you to be more aggressive with the rule and say, "I will film that two-minute video in 30 minutes" or "I will write that blog post in one hour." Almost magically, it will take you closer to getting the work done quicker than you previously imagined. The first time you do a video, it might take 35 minutes instead of 30, but you've already knocked off nearly two and a half hours from your original three! That's a whole 150 minutes to dedicate to something else.

This one is truly brilliant so definitely give it a go!

THE CURSE OF TOO MANY IDEAS

In her book *Big Magic*, Liz Gilbert talks about how ideas are real and alive. She believes that if an idea comes to you and if you don't act on it, it will find a more receptive body. She shares the example of how this happened to her. She had an idea for a book, but was doing other work and got distracted. She then met someone who was writing that **exact** book. Instead of feeling bitter that someone had stolen her idea, she was delighted the idea had found a receptive home.

If you're inundated with lots of ideas about what you could do in your business and you know this becomes a distraction, this is how to deal with it.

Get a notebook and call it your 'Idea Journal'. Whenever you get an idea, instead of thinking you have to act on it immediately, write it down so you don't forget about it and 'park it'. You can come back to it later, but putting it in a holding pattern for a while means you don't get derailed from the task at hand.

Too many ideas can be a self-sabotage strategy. Chasing new ideas all the time becomes a distraction and stops you from building momentum in your business because you never finish what you start. I know what it's like. I have hundreds of ideas, all the time. And it took me a long time to realise that it's not a curse. That said, we all have to become good custodians of the ideas we're already working on. And that means giving them time and space to be implemented.

Constantly chasing after new ideas without finishing existing ones is a fool-proof way to get poor results when you have tiny time, because you're not focusing on your priorities.

SET UP OFFICE HOURS

This simple two-minute trick will make a massive difference to your productivity, especially if you work from home like I do. Define your office hours and stick to them! You get extra brownie points for putting it on paper! Earth shattering, right?

I know it's not that profound. However, this strategy has helped me focus my mind and attention, as well as establish boundaries within the home. Writing down my office hours reminds me of when I do work and when I don't. And that is invaluable when you work in the same building that you live the rest of your life where the tendency can be to pop into the office and keep working!

Having office hours is a great reminder that this is a work place. Too often, working from the kitchen table or a home office can be seen by others as 'not really working'. I hear so many stories where people complain that friends and family pop in for an impromptu coffee when they're working. They hate to say no so their time is devoured by constant interruptions and loose boundaries.

We'll talk more about setting boundaries in the Play Principle.

SNEAKY DISTRACTIONS

Getting distracted is part and parcel of business and life. I am easy to distract. I get a thought in my head and think 'I'd better google that'. Before you know it, I've spent 15 minutes surfing the net!

Between emails, social media, children, boredom and frustration, it can be easy (too easy) to get off-target fast. This happens to me all the time. And it is a struggle. I switch off all social media when I am creating content and doing the important work. But there's always the temptation to switch Facebook back on and see what people are up to. I remember a time I felt blocked and unable to create great content. I made the connection that I was consuming too much content and it was blocking my creativity.

If you know you get distracted easily, set up simple routines that allow you to get your work done but still feed the beast inside you that wants to google! Use a timer and do your work for 30 minutes and then allow yourself a five-minute break. (Use a timer for this too.)

Set a specific time to check your social media and stick to it as much as you can. I installed an app on my phone to see how many times I looked at it and I was astounded. I could not believe it when, in one day, I logged into the phone 85 times! That was a wakeup call. Initially, I justified it because 'I'm running a business'. Then the immediate counter-thought was: *am I running a business or is it running me?* So I set myself a time (normally twice a day) to check social media and email. I allocate 15 to 20 minutes so I can get my fill, then I go back to the important work. This does not always work, but it's something I'm conscious of doing and committed to improving. I'm also keenly aware of modelling healthy phone habits with the kids!

The bottom line is: if you want your work to make an impact and a difference, you can't allow yourself to be distracted.

TO PROCRASTINATE OR NOT?

If you're a master procrastinator, ask yourself the reason behind it. Why do you keep doing it? What are you hiding from? What does procrastinating do for you?

When we choose to not do something, we are benefiting from the not doing. Procrastinating is the symptom, not the cause, so it's important to get to the bottom of it and understand why you do it. Do you hate the work? Does it have to be done by you? Can you delegate it?

When you have tiny time, procrastinating is a great threat, so when you do catch yourself, ask why. Procrastinating is a clever self-sabotage strategy and it needs to be nipped in the bud!

Do, Ditch or Delegate

This is a big deal for most entrepreneurs and business owners. You have so much to do and so many ideas. Where do you start?

I went to a conference in London a couple of years ago and one of the audience members asked the guest speaker, "I'm doing all this. What *else* should I be doing?"

And I loved the response...

"Instead of asking what else you can do, ask yourself: *what can I start saying no to?*"

This is the heart of the matter. We tiny timers cannot do it all. We have to be more discerning about how we spend our time and the work we choose to do. This is why I spent a long time refining my business model (as discussed in the Profit Principle) to make sure I was only doing the work that made a difference and not spreading myself too thin. I made choices to retire certain programs because they were not profitable or a good use of my time.

When it comes to your task list, you need three words.

Do, ditch and delegate!

Create a list of all the things you do in business and determine what **must be done by you** (do), what can be **binned** (ditch) and what **someone else can do** for you (delegate). Here's a list of possible tasks:

- Write weekly blog
- Film video
- Record podcast
- Answer customer emails
- Create slideshows for webinars
- Delete files from the computer
- Bookkeeping every month
- Review the week's activities
- Social media posting
- Sort out home insurance
- Gifts for family members
- Invite podcast guests
- Send weekly newsletter

I remember my coach telling me that I was doing too much. The problem was it fed my inner martyr. 'I can do it all' was my mantra. But in reality, I was burning myself out and piling too much on.

When you have a solid and simple business model, your task list is naturally reduced. But there will still be a lot to do. That is when you have to decide what to do yourself and get the help you need.

OUTSOURCING

So you've done the list, you've decided what to ditch and do. Now let's talk about delegating. This is something I highly recommend, but first you need to be 100% clear on the result you want to achieve and then make sure everything you are doing is geared to that.

You may wish to hire a team member, or if that's too big a step for you right now, maybe because you don't want the responsibility of being an employer, you're better starting with outsourcing. It is less risky and allows you to experiment with understanding what you need and build slowly.

I've had a number of VAs (virtual assistants) in my business and my number one tip is this:

Start with one task!

That might be updating your weekly blog, uploading videos, editing podcast episodes, replying to emails or doing your bookkeeping. Keep it simple to start with, otherwise you will potentially overload the new team member. They may have strengths in one particular area, but not another, and you need to find out what those are instead of ditching them because of one weakness. I did this. I asked too much of one assistant and it didn't end well.

On the positive side, it means I'm a lot more cautious about what I ask people to do for me, and can assess their strengths much better. It is **highly unlikely** you will find one person to do all you need. It is far more realistic to assume you will need one or two or more people.

I'm a big fan of Daniel Priestley and have been fortunate to spend time with him at events. He advises that every small business should have three staff. One for operations, one for sales and one administrator. For each additional staff member, you can add on approximately 50k of revenue.

This approach makes sense because the problem every small business owner has is that their time is finite. Even with tiny time and all the strategies I'm sharing with you to maximise your productivity, your time is still limited. The last thing you want to do is spend the precious time you do have replying to emails, sending your bio to a podcast guest or submitting a guest blog. Get someone else to do these for you!

You need to focus on the high-value activities in your business. Sales is a high-value activity. Only delegate this once you have nailed your offer, you are getting a flood of leads you can't service and you can hire someone you trust to do a portion of the calls for you. My top tip for this is to always get them recorded so you can ensure they are selling with the highest integrity and not making false promises to get the sale... (I have heard some stories!)

I know delegating can be a scary prospect. *What if they don't do it* **exactly** *the way I want?* Quite honestly, they won't because they're not you, but you can mitigate this by having strong standard operating procedures where you can communicate clearly how you like things done right from the beginning.

If you don't like how someone does the work, you need to ensure you set expectations. People are not mind-readers. It's your job to articulate clearly what you are asking of them. It can take time but it's well worth it. Think of all the time you'll save!

When looking for support:

- Be clear on what you need help with
- Look for referrals rather than cold-calling — word of mouth is a far better way to find a trusted team member!
- Start off with one task only and build slowly
- Be clear in your expectations and make sure you communicate regularly
- Create standard operating procedures so everyone is on the same page
- Use a tool like Asana or Basecamp to stay in communication— which also saves you having to read chain emails!

Even if your business is not making enough money right now to warrant hiring an assistant, think about how you can outsource some of the tasks that are time-drainers. Outsourcing can be a fantastic way to build a big-impact business without massive overheads. As long as you do it thoughtfully and strategically.

YOU'VE PLANNED, YOU'VE DONE, NOW REVIEW

One of the mantras we lived by when I was in training and

development was 'plan, do, and review'. We plan the work, we do the work... Then we review the work. Taking the time to review where you're at and the progress you're making is a key part of the 90-day planning strategy. There's no point in planning and doing if you don't take a little time every week or month to review.

The review needs to take into account your:

- Money
- Marketing
- Clients
- What's working?
- What's not working?
- Enjoyment factor

In the spirit of keeping my business simple, I use the same approach for reviewing. I recommend allocating 15 minutes at the end of each week to review.

When it comes to your **money**, you need to know what you've brought in and what's gone out. If you do this on a monthly basis, it's so much easier to get your accounts sorted and your head clear on where you need to focus than if you do what the majority of business owners do: see what the accountant says once a year.

Look at the **marketing** you did that week. What was effective and what was a waste of time? What created traction? Is it social media advertising or sharing in groups? Keep asking: what's working? Then ditch what isn't!

Keep abreast of the work you're doing with your **clients**. Keep a tracker (a simple Excel sheet is enough) so you know what you're doing with each one. Having an ad-hoc approach is fine when you only have a handful of clients. But when you get more, you need somewhere to jot down thoughts and actions after calls so you stay focused.

Ask yourself: *am I enjoying what I'm doing?* We'll talk about this in the Play Principle too. Having **fun** is such a critical element of your business and life! If you're not having fun, look to see what's happening. I used to get triggered by others because I thought: *they're having so much more fun than me.* It was crazy to be bothered by this because my own level of fun was within my control. So I made an intention to bring more fun to my life. More fun with how I worked. More fun with the children. And that made a big difference!

If you allow time to review your business every week or month, you will be able to course-correct. I don't advise leaving it to every quarter or worse every year to know what to start, stop or continue doing.

ACCOUNTABILITY

Holding yourself accountable is one of the most powerful strategies that will move you closer to achieving your goals. It has a greater impact than the latest marketing tactic or the new must-have tech tool. It's also an activity that can make some people shudder and others nod empathetically that it's exactly what they need, but then hide when it's time to commit.

In business, we have an abundance of information and ideas. We don't need more information. We need implementation and this is where accountability serves you. If you start each year with lots of exciting goals (some loftier than others maybe!) that you can't even remember within a couple of weeks, chances are you just missed out on a crucial portion of what really makes the difference: accountability. Whether that means you hold yourself accountable, you get someone else to help you or you enrol the help of a coach.

I recommend a daily tracker to help you stay on target. I want to know I am working on the right things in my business. Using a simple spreadsheet, I log what I have done each day. This takes just five minutes, but is invaluable when I do my end-of-week review, because I can see if I have used my time meaningfully or frittered it away. You can allow a margin of 'fritter-bility', but if you want a successful tiny-time business, you do have to know in detail where your time is being spent.

I appreciate this can be hard to do for yourself, so get yourself a coach or an accountability buddy to help you stay on track!

If you allow time to review your business every week or month, you will be able to course-correct. I don't advise leaving it to every quarter or worse every year to know what to start, stop or continue doing.

THE PRODUCTIVITY PRINCIPLE IN A NUTSHELL

As you can see, being productive with your time is essential when you have a tiny-time business. Whatever tiny time looks like for you, your main aim is to make the most of the time you have. Once you have your business model sorted out (which we covered in the Profit Principle), then focus on creating processes and routines that make time your friend, not your enemy.

When you are working in your business, ask yourself:

- Is this activity moving me closer to my goals?
- Am I doing the work that matters?
- Am I focused?
- If I'm procrastinating or becoming distracted, why am I allowing this?

Tiny Steps, Done Consistently

When it comes to being productive and doing the work that makes a difference, the best thing you can be is consistent. Even if you have only had time to write one blog post, that's fine. It's important to be kind to yourself and your circumstances if your tiny time shrinks on you and you don't have any time to do anything. This is why scheduling your time and getting clear on your deliverables makes such a huge impact.

Each tiny step creates a ripple effect. Please don't dismiss them just because they are tiny. Your tiny-time business will thrive because of those tiny steps when you are consistent with them.

To run a profitable business in 20 hours a week, being productive means you:

- Declutter your mind
- Have laser-like focus
- Have clearly defined working time
- Hold yourself accountable
- Delegate for growth
- Hold strong boundaries

Now let's move on to the fun stuff — The Play Principle!

SECTION 6: THE PLAY PRINCIPLE

We don't stop playing because we grow old; we grow old because we stop playing.

— George Bernard Shaw

The Play Principle is about how we show up in our business, how much fun and enjoyment we bring to our work, and how we treat ourselves. It's about how we manage our energy and state of mind so we can be at our best. Ironically, when I share the four principles of tiny time, people often laugh when I talk about play, as if play and business are incompatible! It makes me even more determined to help people bring more play into their businesses and lives!

Your business is an expression of you, a vehicle for your talents, skills and passions. If what you are doing is not fun and you don't enjoy it 70% of the time or more, this is a clear signal that something needs to change. I want you to love your business like I do (most of the time!), enjoy yourself and infuse happiness into how you work, because doing this amplifies your results and feels good. (Best ever reason to do something!)

One of my coaches once told me 'you are not your business'. It was like flicking a switch and the light coming on. I had been having a hard time. Money was tight and I was struggling to attract clients because my mindset was focused on lack. In that moment, I realised I had allowed the state of my business to reflect my self-worth. Thankfully, I knew that was a slippery slope! I determined to separate myself from my business.

If business is not going well, it does not mean you are unworthy or not valuable. It simply means you have lost your way and not working in a way that aligns with you. All work and no play makes you exhausted and burnt out. And then you can't serve anyone!

Your business does not need to succeed for you to be a valuable person. You already are! In this section, I talk about how to care for yourself, the inner work and the outer work you can do to keep you in a state of high energy, remain positive and make time to play.

CHAPTER 25: SELF-CARE — THE INNER WORK

MINDSET

Your mindset is one of the most powerful assets you have and your success lies in your ability to choose how you show up in the world, your life and your business. Having your own business requires intense personal development. What you struggle with in your day-to-day life becomes magnified when you have your own business. If you have money issues, they will multiply. If you don't like the idea of doing sales, you will have to overcome this to be successful. If you find it hard to meet people and build relationships, you will have to shift your thinking to allow you to do this easily. It does not mean you change who you are, but there will be things you need to get comfortable with so you and your business can succeed.

When I started my business, I thought I had a relatively healthy mindset towards challenges and had a certain resilience. I've overcome significant hurdles in my personal life, including marrying out of my faith despite considerable opposition. Adversity is no stranger to me. However, I did not factor in quite how much being a business owner would push me out of my comfort zone. Every step I have shared with you in this book about how to make your business work in your tiny time has been part of my experience. I'm showing you how to do it because I did the exact opposite and paid the price.

As you read through the self-care section, think of these actions as mindset-strengthening. They are designed to help you get stronger and more resilient when you run your business. If running your own business was easy, everyone would do it. You're still here because this is important to you and you want to be the master of your life, take control of your financial destiny and share your message with the people you're here to serve.

It might feel indulgent to spend time on your self-care when you have clients to sign and bills to pay but there's a reason why play is crucial in the tiny time approach. Self-care is not about having a massage once a week. It's about nurturing yourself, your mind, body and spirit so you can show up strong. Your mindset is the glue that binds everything together.

TRUST AND VALUE YOURSELF

I can trace the downtime and low periods in my business to the times when I lost my self-confidence. When I stopped trusting in my abilities and focused on what I couldn't do instead of what I do well. (Is it too much to say brilliantly?!)

A few months ago, my eldest came home with a bad result in his spelling test. That one test result shook his confidence and he stopped trusting himself. He lost his self-belief, started acting up and would get angry quickly. I could see this struggle was playing on his mind and I had to help him. I know how damaging it can be to not trust yourself anymore. I can't shield my kids from getting knocked around by life, but I can help them build their resilience muscles. We worked on his spelling, encouraged his reading, and praised his handwriting and maths (which come easily to him). Slowly, bit by bit, his confidence grew and he started to relax. He's only little so this will be an ongoing project.

I don't claim any miracles when it comes to children. Next week, it will be something else!

This is the crucial bit I want you to take from this. My son got stuck when he focused on what he could not do and disregarded what he does well. There will be things you have to do in business that you're not good at, but there is plenty you are brilliant at. Keep reminding yourself of your strengths and work on whatever needs improvement that will move your business forward, like your sales skills.

When I focused on what I couldn't do, I ignored my abilities, skills and gifts, pushing them aside and focusing on my hang-ups. I stopped valuing my skills and others stopped valuing me too. Prospects who had said yes suddenly said no. The money was running out. It was a reflection of what was happening to me internally. Why would anyone value me and what I could do for them if I did not believe in myself? Would you hire someone like that?

And the thing is you never have to utter a word. It's in your energy. The way you hold your body. The way you absent yourself from the things that will move you forward, like attending networking meetings, events or conferences. If you show up in a sales conversation full of your own doubt, your prospect will sense it and it will repel them. They won't even know why! If you want a profitable business in less than 20 hours a week, you must value yourself. My business took off exponentially when I (finally) took stock of what I and my clients had achieved, and truly began to value myself.

Here's an activity that helped me tremendously and I highly recommend it.

Make a list of all the clients you have helped and write down the result you helped them create. Stack them high. Think of every single client you've ever worked with — free or paid — and write it all down. Look at the testimonials you have. And if you don't have testimonials, I would encourage doing a number of free sessions and asking for a testimonial in return, so others can see the transformation you create.

Then stick that piece of paper somewhere prominent and look at it **every day** to remind yourself how awesome you are!

Your confidence and self-belief will act like a shining light for your clients and the people you are here to serve.

STOP COMPARING YOURSELF TO OTHERS

When I first started my business, I was a sucker for everything on social media. I soaked it all up and wondered why I felt awful. I believed everything people wrote and it used to burn my soul when I read about someone making a big ball of money in a crazy short time. All I could think was: Why not me? It took a long time to realise I was naïve to believe what everyone was saying. I'd been too harsh on myself. People share their highlights on social media and websites. We don't share that we were bawling for the last hour before filming that video. We don't share that we're worried about how to pay our bills.

So today, you are going to do something that your soul will thank you for. You are about to let go of comparison-itis! If you keep comparing yourself to others and finding yourself lacking, it's time to give yourself a break. When you compare yourself to others, you're on to a loser because someone will always be better, prettier, thinner, more successful <enter hang-up here> than you!

(Or you'll become vain and realise you are oh-so-much better than them!)

I believe we are here for a unique purpose. When we compare ourselves to others, it's like a slap in the face of the Divine that brought us here. Comparing yourself to someone else means you take your eye off the ball, feel hideous and disregard your journey. Even if someone's life looks amazing, everyone has their struggles. By comparing yourself, you put them on a pedestal. Others may make more money than you. They may have more followers or a bigger email list. It does not matter. You are not in competition with them. You are only ever competing with the person you were yesterday.

Take a moment to think who you were six months ago. How have you changed? How have you moved forward? What makes you proud? The Universe is abundant. There is enough for everyone. If someone makes a lot of money, it does not mean there is less money available to you. There is enough for us all.

Next time you find yourself comparing yourself to someone else, repeat these words...

I am not in competition with anybody else — I hope we all make it.

This is one of the most generous acts of self-care you can do, because nothing will derail you more than believing others are better than you.

FORGIVE YOURSELF

Forgiving yourself is a powerful gift you can give yourself for anything and everything.

- Woke up late and snapped at your partner? Forgive yourself.
- Working to a deadline and annoyed with yourself for leaving it till the last minute? Forgive yourself.
- Angry at yourself for not making enough progress in your business? Forgive yourself.

You are always doing your best with what you know and what you have. If you continually beat yourself up for not being good enough, or not knowing enough, or thinking of all the 'shoulds' in your business and life, please stop!

Forgive yourself by repeating this statement internally...

I forgive you, I'm sorry and I love you.

This comes from the Hawaiian Huna method. It allows you to take responsibility for what happened but also affirm your love for yourself. I love its power and simplicity. Try it and see how amazing it feels to let yourself off the hook!

RAISE YOUR VIBE

If you want to achieve a particular outcome, like making 10k or losing 10lbs, your first task is to raise the frequency of your energy to match the energy of the goal. What does this mean? All physical reality is made up of vibrations of energy. Each and every single thought and emotion you have vibrates a frequency. Some resonate high on the scale like love, joy, contentment and peace; some low like guilt, shame, envy and fear. Everything vibrates at a particular frequency. This means you will find it easier to reach the goals you have, attain what you aspire to have, connect with the people you want in your life and business when your energy matches the vibration of the goal or desire. Think of it as tuning your radio to find the right station. If you're looking for 100FM, you won't find it on long wave radio!

When you set an income goal or call in your ideal client multiplied by 10, you cannot attract that into your life (through your intentions and actions) if you are resonating at a lower frequency. For example, a lower frequency of fear or worry.

If you want to make 10k, you cannot be in the energy of making 1k or even 5k. If you want to lose 10lbs, you can't achieve that if your energy is resonating at the frequency of 'I'll be fine if I just lose 2lbs'. Your intention and energy must be a match. Your job is to embody what it feels like to make 10k or lose 10lbs.

In your journal, ask yourself what making 10k would do for you. What would it allow you to do? How would you feel when you made 10k? Describe it in as much detail as possible, then sit in the energy of already achieving it. Scan your body to see how it feels in your toes, your fingers, your spine, your head, your chest and all over your body. Take four deep breaths to breathe the outcome in.

This is a great exercise to start your day, because once you sit in the energy of already achieving something, you run the day as if it is already done. You keep the same feelings running through you. When I think about a money goal and imagine it is done, I see myself playing fully in the moment with my children instead of constantly checking the phone. I see myself doing the laundry with a light heart! I see myself working with my clients and loving every moment of it. I see my appointment diary filling up with qualified prospects!

When you raise the frequency of your energy to meet the frequency of your goal, you can't help but achieve it.

If the goal you set feels too pie-in-the-sky, bring it down to what feels like a stretch goal but still do-able. I don't believe in telling yourself you're going to make a million dollars next year when you're only making $25k right now. That kind of thinking doesn't set you up for success. It derails you and prevents you from taking actions that will move you closer to the goal. If the goal feels too big, your energy will reject the goal and there will be no internal alignment.

When I set my income goal to 10k a month, I know I can achieve that because I have done that before. Setting a goal of 100k a month is a stretch because I haven't done that — yet! How about doubling your goal or upgrading in increments instead? Instead of aiming for a million, aim for 35k or double your annual income to 50k.

How you raise your energy frequency will be unique to you. I love to dance, meditate, cook, read, do yoga, go for a walk and tickle my children. If people aren't returning your calls or say no in your sales conversations, check in with yourself and question what kind of energy you're showing up with.

It's not always about your strategies, but the energy you use to implement them.

CELEBRATE

One of the most important things you can do for yourself and your inner world is to celebrate every single achievement and milestone you reach in your business. Whether it's a chocolate bar at the end of a tough week or a new necklace when you sign a new client, it doesn't matter. What matters is you take the time to recognise and appreciate everything you are doing.

Some people only celebrate when they hit a big milestone like an income goal. Some people put off celebrating because they don't think it's noteworthy or they change the goalposts. I prefer the small and often approach *as well as* celebrating the big wins. If I have done a sales conversation and I feel good about it (it doesn't have to be a sale), that's a win. If I have a great call with a client, that's a win.

Create opportunities and ways to celebrate and recognise your wins...it will make the journey so much sweeter!

That's the inner work. Now let's do the outer work!

Some people only celebrate when they hit a big milestone like an income goal. Some people put off celebrating because they don't think it's noteworthy or they change the goalposts. I prefer the small and often approach as well as celebrating the big wins.

CHAPTER 26: PRACTICAL SELF- CARE — THE OUTER WORK

In this section, I share simple practical ways you can practise self-care. You don't have to do them all. Pick one that resonates and begin integrating it into your daily life. I am sharing with you what has worked for me and my clients, but I don't do them all. I wouldn't have the time!

Looking after yourself is essential in business. You cannot afford to burn out. You won't be able to serve your clients or look after your loved ones if your cup is empty.

YOUR MORNING ROUTINE

How do you start the day? Do you fall out of bed into a day-long Krypton-Factor-style assault course where you're constantly avoiding, jumping over or crawling under obstacles? Or do you step into the day with intention and calm?

I know what you're thinking... If you didn't have a great night's sleep, the kids are jumping all over you or your dog whined all night because he can't sleep at the foot of your bed, waking up feeling serene is a bit far-fetched. In our house, we play musical beds. I never know which bed I'll end up in by the morning!

But setting yourself up for success in the morning does not have to take hours. It always tickles me when someone suggests meditating for two hours. That is not my world, not with three young children! We have to make this work for us. What I am talking about is something that will take you just 15 minutes to do. Even if you do this a few hours after the kids have woken up, that's okay. Whatever you decide on, ground yourself before rushing headlong into activity.

For me, this is taking at least 15 minutes to get ready for the day, broken into three chunks:

5 minutes: Stretch

5 minutes: Inspire

5 minutes: Intent

You can do these for longer, but when you're pushed for time or just want a routine you can do easily, I recommend starting with five minutes each.

In your five-minute **stretch**, move your body. Don't let your body get creaky. Move it as much as you can because that will help you get more oxygen to your brain too. Stretch out your limbs. I love yoga so I end up doing a few cat stretches, downward dog or warrior. If you're not sure what to do, search for 'five-minute stretches' on YouTube and you'll pick up easy routines. (What did we do without YouTube?) The idea is to stretch yourself out so you feel loose and limber. Imagine you're about to start a race — you don't want to be tight and tense.

For the next five minutes, you read, watch or listen someth that will **inspire** you! This could be a spiritual text, a book that uplifts you or a video of somebody who inspires you. I love reading books and watching videos by people like Wayne Dyer, Kyle Cease, Florence Scovel Shinn, Oprah, Abraham Hicks, Rebecca Campbell or Stuart Wilde. Doing this uplifts your soul so you feel excited and passionate about your life! There are some mornings when I just don't 'feel it'. When you're feeling underwhelmed about what you do, downhearted about the progress you're making, or worried about money stuff, this ritual will help lift you out of the funk.

For the last five minutes, set your **intention**. What word or phrase do you want to use as your anchor for the day? Is it peace? Is it service? Is it abundance? Is it focus? You can do this for just your work or for your whole day, including your relationships, your fun, your spirit... It's up to you!

Spending 15 minutes to pump yourself up will give you a boost rather than stumbling into your day and wondering what you'll do. I've done both and I know which one I prefer. A morning routine can help so much.

And funnily enough, you don't need massive actions to make an impact. By that I mean, you don't have to take big leaps every single day to hit your targets. Small changes can make a huge difference.

DRINK A LITRE OF WATER (AT LEAST)

Water hydrates your mind, body and spirit. You already know this but for some reason it's something people find hard to do. I'm one of those, so at the beginning of this year, I made one resolution. To start drinking 600ml of water (the size of my water

for a month. Then to increase it to 1200ml by the

mprovements and can see when I have been drinking. My skin is clearer and I have much more energy. My brain works better too! On the other hand, when I haven't drunk enough water, I feel sluggish, tired and mentally drained.

CREATE A VISION AND FEELING BOARD

A vision board is a tool you can use to create your deepest desires and make them real. It helps you define what you want in your life and put your focus on it. Making a vision board requires you to take time out and think about what exactly you want to create. Sometimes we think we know or we have a vague idea, but we don't know for sure. But if you want to make something happen, you need to be specific. The Universe loves specificity!

Here's how to get started. Take 15 minutes to jot down up to 10 things you want to make real in the next three years. It could be a dream home, a trip to Hawaii, a sleek office space, your published book or an incredible family holiday in Australia. Get some magazines and cut out pictures or words that represent what you want in life and business. It could be cars, homes, gorgeous clients or fab food — pick what inspires you, motivates you and gets your heart racing!

Before you start sticking pictures on a sheet of cardboard, set your intention that this is your dream vision. Take a couple of deep breaths into your belly, let them out and get sticking!

To add extra oomph to your vision board, include your achievements, so when you look at it, you see what you have already accomplished and are more receptive to the unrealised dreams. I learnt this vision board nuance from Rebecca Campbell, author of *Rise Sister Rise*. Her suggestion makes a huge difference to the energy of the board.

Once you're done, place it somewhere you can see it easily and keep reaffirming your dream. My son loved creating a vision board recently during his mindfulness class. His board now hangs proudly next to mine!

SAY NO

One of the most common questions I am asked is: *what else should I do?* It's an interesting question based on the assumption we should be doing more. I prefer thinking about what else I could stop doing.

I used to run a group accountability program but it wasn't profitable. I stuck with it for a long time even though it didn't make any sense at all. When I finally decided to close the program, I was sad because I had enjoyed it but it was also a relief. Ironically, I held onto it longer than I should have because it brought in some money, but within one month of shutting it down, I tripled my monthly income.

When you ask yourself what else you should do, your belief centres on not doing enough. This leads you to the idea that the more you do, the more successful you will be. But that's crazy thinking, because you have tiny time. You can't do more! So instead of trying to do more, look at what you can stop. And start saying no.

No to requests for 'a quick coffee' where someone wants to pick your brain.

No to the client who always wants you to do little extras.

No to that customer who keeps asking for a discount.

Even no to friends who want to pop in for a quick chat when you're working.

Saying no means establishing boundaries around what you're willing and not willing to do.

FIRE YOURSELF (FOR THE DAY)

When was the last time you gave yourself a day off? A proper day off with no emails, no clients and no social media? Taking time off from your business is essential for you to stay fresh and engaged with your work. It means you take the time to rest and recuperate. If you're always doing, you will find more things to do, but if you make a conscious decision to take time off, you build that into your schedule and plan your work accordingly.

When you create your 90-day plan, factor in your holidays and days off. What gets scheduled gets done!

EARTH YOURSELF

When something happens that makes you wobble (a hurtful comment, a criticism, a failed product launch — anything that shakes you), find something to steady you so you don't stray from your path.

Go outside. Take off your shoes. Place your feet on actual earth... not concrete but soil. Plant your feet and imagine yourself connecting to the centre of the earth. Imagine there's a piece of string running from the top of your head right down to your toes, straight through the earth and right down to its core. Feel the stability. Nothing can rock you. You are the rock.

When you feel overwhelmed with business, life or family, do this for just a few minutes and you will feel its power.

SET BOUNDARIES WITH CLIENTS

I have had many conversations with clients about setting appropriate boundaries. Most of the time, the problem lies in non-existent boundaries!

I worked with a client a few years ago who felt compelled to answer prospect queries at all hours. She was worried that if she didn't reply within an hour, she would lose the business. It was exhausting her and she was worried, because it was setting a precedent that she was available at all hours. Clients then took advantage.

When you are self-employed, it does not mean you are at the beck and call of your clients and customers. You are entitled to downtime and you should get it!

Encroaching on boundaries can include family members disregarding your work time, people popping in for coffee when you're working, or clients asking for last-minute 'favours'.

Here are two simple strategies you can do with your clients:

1. Automatic autoreply on your email

This will take you two minutes to set up! Your email service has an 'Out of Office' functionality for when you're on holiday. Instead of using it only at holiday time, set it up to work all the time. This is my automatic message:

Thank you for your message, I have received it and I will get back to you as soon as possible.

I check emails at certain intervals and for limited periods of time, so you may not get an immediate response. If your enquiry is urgent, please call me on xxxxxx.

I really appreciate your patience and look forward to connecting with you again soon.

All the best!

Yasmin

This approach sets out clear boundaries. When you do this, you teach people how you want to be treated. Depending on the nature of your business and your own preferences, you may choose to leave out the option of calling you and including your phone number. It's up to you... It's your business!

2. Establish boundaries in your welcome pack and terms and conditions

In the Profit Principle, I recommend providing a welcome pack for your new clients. In the welcome pack, let them know your working hours, planned holidays and how you can be contacted. When you establish boundaries, to begin with, you will not struggle unless you allow too much flexibility!

If you find you're the one who breaks boundaries and lets people do that too, you need to close this energy leak. Time to reflect. Why are you afraid to say no? What do you think your refusal will mean for that person? Are you worried about how they will react?

You teach people how you want to be treated. If you're still struggling with family and friends, or the 'can I pick your brain?' people, re-read the Say No section!

SAGE SMUDGING

This is similar to the decluttering we talked about in the Productivity Principle. When you clear the clutter from your environment, cleanse the energy of the environment as well, by lighting dried sage. Sage smudging is an ancient practice that you do mindfully to clear any negativity.

If you've never done this before, you will need a bunch of dried sage, matches and a fireproof container. As you light the sage, set the intention to cleanse the space. Once the sage starts to smoke, walk around your home with it, blowing the smoke around windows and doors. You can also waft the smoke around yourself to cleanse your energy.

When I do this, I feel lighter and freer immediately. Sometimes, it's the simple act of setting an intention and doing something mindfully that makes the shift.

Caution: Take care with matches, especially with little ones around. Light your sage stick over the fireproof bowl so no lit herbs fall on the floor.

EAT GREENS!

To live a great quality of life, you need bags of energy. Energy for your business, energy for your family, your loved ones, your hobbies and everything else in between.

Too often, the problem is not our lack of enthusiasm, but poor choice of fuel. If you had a high-end luxury car, would you put cheap fuel into it? Would you let the average mechanic get her hands on your pride and joy? Not likely! But when it comes to our own bodies, when we're feeling tired or listless, we reach for the quick-fix, like caffeine or sugar, even knowing we'll crash within 30 minutes of consuming it!

Here's what to do instead...

Eat more greens!

One Christmas, I asked for a Nutribullet and it has been a godsend! It's a great way to get oodles of green goodness into you without having to eat copious amounts of fruit and veg. Don't get me wrong, I love veg, but have you seen how much you have to eat compared to drinking it? Using a Nutribullet instead of a juicer means I still get the fibre too, but you don't need an appliance like the Nutribullet to make healthier choices.

Drink more water and crowd out poor choices with healthy options and you will soon boost your energy levels.

STAY AWAY FROM ENERGY VAMPIRES

Have you ever spoken to someone and found yourself looking for the exit within a matter of minutes? Energy vampires will suck the life out of you if you let them. This could be the client you shouldn't have signed or the friend who is a Debbie Downer all the time. This is not about shaking off friends who are going through a tough time, but about being discerning about who gets your precious time. I love having deep conversations with people and spending time with people who inspire me. My immediate family, parents, sister, brother and his family, in-laws and cousins; they are my chief inspirers. Then I have my friends and my soul sisters, my work colleagues, and the people I connect with on social media.

I make a conscious decision to stay away from people who choose to blame others all the time, play the victim or are unwilling to take steps to change what does not serve them.

When my daughter has a tantrum about her socks touching her feet (a constant theme in our house), I ask, "Do you want to take them off?" When she says she doesn't, I tell her that if she's not willing to change what is in her control, she has no right to complain about it. I feel sorry for the child. She's only five!

DO A DIGITAL DETOX

Switching off the phone and stepping away from social media is good for your health. Study after study shows that staying switched on affects our physical and mental health. Allocate a day each week where you don't look at your phone. Put it in a drawer and step away.

You'll see just how addicted you are, when you start getting the shakes! Which means it's even more important to take time away from your device. Just because we have smartphones and can be available 24/7 doesn't mean we should. I'm definitely a work in progress with this one!

THANKFULNESS

Whenever I feel down or I'm in a funk that I can't shake off, I remember all the things I have and how lucky I am. When things are tough, it can feel hard to be thankful, but it will lift your spirits and the feeling of joy in your body.

I like to do this at bedtime with my children. We say a big thank you to God for our warm house, our warm beds, hot food in our tummies, all the cuddles we had during the day. We keep going for as long as we can. And the best bit? When they go to sleep, they're falling asleep with gratitude on their lips. (In the interests of complete transparency, this doesn't always happen!)

It doesn't matter if you're having a crappy day or an awesome one. Just get thanking like crazy! Because when you feel the joy, you attract more of it!

GET 12 HUGS A DAY

According to Virginia Satir, author and family therapist, we need a minimum of four hugs a day for survival, eight hugs for maintenance, and twelve for growth. I don't think anything beats the feeling of being supported in a warm embrace. If you've not been getting your basic quota, you're in need of cuddles!

This has a powerful effect in your business too. When you feel nurtured, loved and supported, your best work pours out of you. You attract the best clients and you're paid well. All because you took the time to make sure you filled your quota of hugs!

MAKE TIME TO PLAY

When I was a child, I used to love going to the playground and playing on the swings. Now I get to do it with my children! I love to play on the swings, skip down the road and make believe. I get roped into playing school, but my daughter is a strict teacher! My eldest son loves it when we play ball together. And the baby loves to play hide and seek.

Making time to play helps you to release your inner child from the day-to-day demands of life and business. It reminds you that you are more than your business. It lifts your mood, helps you to be fully present and rejuvenates you for your work.

It doesn't matter what kind of play you do, but to be true to its essence, it's an activity that has no outcome. It just is!

GO TO BED 30 MINS EARLIER

Sleep is one of the most important gifts we can give to ourselves. As a mum of three, sleep deprivation is part and parcel of life. I deeply cherish the nights when I can sleep soundly. I do not enjoy disturbed sleep courtesy of a teething baby. (But then who does?)

Getting enough rest is crucial, not just for your physical health, but your mental health too. Sleep deprivation can create so much stress and illness in our bodies, and dramatically reduces our concentration. Make rest and sleep a priority in your life and get to bed half an hour earlier than you usually do.

THE PLAY PRINCIPLE IN A NUTSHELL

Play is the one principle that may fall low on your priority list, but I would encourage you to make it a high priority and find time to include it. As you can see in this section, play is not just about having fun. It's about taking care of your inner and outer world.

To run a profitable business in 20 hours a week, play means you:

- Have strong self-belief
- Trust in your value
- Raise your vibe and match the frequency of the people you're here to serve
- Take time off for rest and recovery
- Have fun!

Play is the one principle that may fall low on your priority list, but I would encourage you to make it a high priority and find time to include it. As you can see in this section, play is not just about having fun. It's about taking care of your inner and outer world.

SECTION 7: ROADBLOCKS

Do not judge me by my success, judge me by how many times I fell down and got back up again.

— **Nelson Mandela**

CHAPTER 27: WHAT COULD STOP YOU?

We have covered a lot in this book about how to run a profitable business in 20 hours a week or less. And I know how it goes. You get inspired, you begin to implement, and then you hit a roadblock. Below are some of the common roadblocks you may encounter... as well as how to tackle them.

TOO EASY

There will be a part of you that thinks this 20-hour week business is impossible. It sounds too easy. If it was possible, everybody would be doing it. I understand where your disbelief comes from. There is plenty of evidence and people out there who suggest you need to be working crazy hours to make it big in this world.

I don't want to argue. This book is not about me convincing you this can work for you. This book is about showing you it can be done. You might read this book and still not believe it's possible for you. This boils down to your belief system.

I started this journey because of my circumstances. I wanted to spend time with my babies and not work all the time. Everything I have covered in this book is tried and tested. So it can be done. If you think it sounds too easy to be true, ask yourself why you're resistant to an easier life.

TOO HARD

Conversely, you might be thinking this is all too hard. I promise you it's not, but you have to be willing to go on the journey to see how it could apply to your business. Perhaps you're working 40+ hours and can't see how you will ever work less than 20. That's okay. Why not reduce your hours by five as a first step?

Tiny steps done consistently will create the results you want. Sometimes it's not about the big leaps, but showing up consistently and doing the work. It's not too hard when you know why you want to do it and commit to making it happen.

OVERCOMPLICATED BUSINESS MODEL

One of the most powerful things you can do for your business and sanity is to keep things as simple as possible. A simple way to create profit. A simple way to organise yourself. A simple way to keep track of everything you're doing.

What isn't easily fixed is when your business model is the problem. When you have so many products in your range that you don't even know what you're offering. When your website is like a menu with 15 different starters, 15 main meals and 15 desserts, or you only have one service that you're struggling to sell.

I speak from experience when I say there is no one business model that suits everyone. I have been through so many iterations of mine. Part of me thinks, *Why couldn't I get it right in the first place?* Then the kinder, logical part of me thinks, *This is all part of the journey!* No-one starts a business knowing everything. It doesn't fall into place like magic right from the start. Trial and error is normal. But knowing that your end outcome is a simple and profitable business model allows you to ask great quality questions along the way.

- Is this making the business more complicated?
- Am I serving my clients in the highest way possible if I do this?
- Am I making life harder for myself if I organise my time like this?
- Why am I doing this program if it's not breaking even?

If your business model and working style are too complicated and rigid, you will struggle. Be open to what is evolving and stay curious.

TECHNOLOGY

Technology is one of those areas that can make you want to scream or run and hide. It can be daunting when you don't know what you don't know. It can stop you in your tracks because you know you need to create something like a sequence of emails or a webpage, but you don't know how.

We all have to start somewhere and there are plenty of people out there who can help you. You don't have to do it all! It's useful to know how your website and main systems work, but it doesn't mean you have to DIY it all. When technology threatens to overwhelm and paralyse you, take heart in knowing everything can be figured out. You don't have to do this alone!

What technology to use and how to use it is covered in detail in Tiny Time Business School because I do not want it to be your roadblock. Technology is a powerful enabler. It helps your business work beautifully in tiny time.

PERFECTIONISM

We often spend too long on certain tasks because our inner perfectionist tells us what we have done is not good enough. To be truly effective, you will need to curb this bad boy.

Money loves speed so get used to things not being perfect. Get used to your offers not being 100% right before promoting them. Get used to your videos not being as slick as you would like. Get comfortable with not being perfect, because perfection does not exist! You're merely using it as a procrastination strategy. While this is normal, each time you delay getting your service out to the market, or you keep tweaking the website before launching, you hold yourself back by not living your message or sharing your value.

RESISTANCE TO INVEST IN YOURSELF, YOUR SKILLS OR YOUR GROWTH

Formal education will make you a living.

Self-education will make you a fortune.

— Jim Rohn

Continuously developing your skills is essential for any profession, especially for the small business owner. Learning, refining and honing your skills is paramount to helping you take those leaps and bounds I know you want to make.

One of my earliest mentors Tony Robbins says 'success leaves clues'. When you want to progress in a career, seek out the person who has already achieved that success. When you want to lose 15lbs, find someone who has done that before. When you want your child to sleep through the night, look for someone who can help.

Success leaves clues so think hard about what you want to achieve then find the person who's done it. Learning and developing your skills has to be a priority so you can cut your own learning curve short and avoid costly mistakes. Keep an open mind and stay curious, especially about mistakes.

When I look back over my journey so far, these are the three biggest mistakes I made:

- Not honing in on a specific problem that I could solve

- Not knowing my audience well enough

- Infusing a desperate energy into what I was doing, chasing money and losing trust in myself

If I could turn back time and start again, here's what I would tell myself to focus on:

- Crafting a compelling message
- Knowing and building an audience
- Asking them what they want
- Creating a core offer
- Selling it!
- Rinse and repeat!
- Leverage, leverage and more leverage!

Don't be afraid to invest in yourself, but be wary of investing because you're afraid to miss out. FOMO (fear of missing out) is real but you can avoid it by focusing on what you need to know right now to move your business forward. I advocate 'just in time' learning, not 'just in case'.

To do this effectively, look at where you want the business to go in the next 6 to 12 months, and identify the gaps in your knowledge and skills. Now plug those gaps and ignore everything else!

BEING SUCCESSFUL

This sounds like a crazy block. Why would being successful be a block? We often hear people talking about the fear of failure, but rarely do we acknowledge a fear of success. Deep down, though, we have fears about being successful. And when fears are *very* deep down, we are not aware of how they prevent us taking action that would move us forward.

To tap into what could be holding you back, think about your big vision for the business and your life. When you think about this ultimate vision, there will be a tiny voice of disquiet. It can be almost completely mute, but if you listen closely, it's there. Tap into it and listen to the tiny voice. What is it afraid of? Is it afraid that if you become successful, you won't have time for your family? That you'll have to pay a lot more tax? That the business will grow so much and you will lose your work-life balance? That you'll become a workaholic? That, if you become super busy, you will lose your relationship and be lonely? 'I'll have to pay more tax' is one of the most common negative consequences that stops people, because they use it to limit how much they make.

This is a great exercise to do whenever you set a goal because it helps you bring to the surface underlying beliefs that could be hindering you. Think about what you want to achieve and then the negative consequences of achieving the goal. It can be hard to uncover them to begin with, but I promise you, they are there.

When you're aware of your block, you can create a solution around it, rather than ignore it and allow it to sabotage you. Awareness is everything!

We often hear people talking about the fear of failure, but rarely do we acknowledge a fear of success. Deep down, though, we have fears about being successful. And when fears are very deep down, we are not aware of how they prevent us taking action that would move us forward.

SECTION 8: SUMMARY AND WHAT'S NEXT?

The man who moves a mountain begins by carrying away small stones.

— Confucius

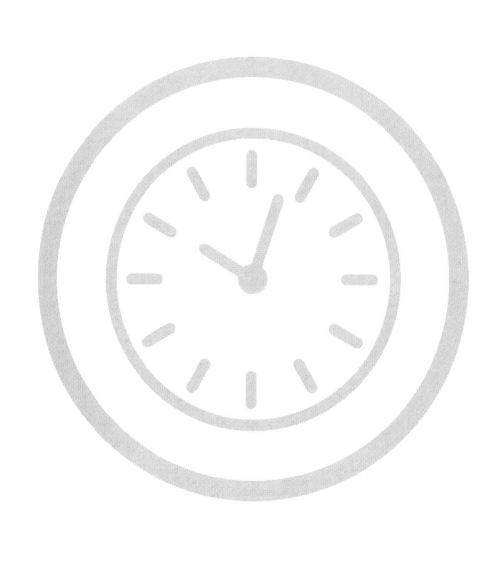

CHAPTER 28: SUMMARY

Tiny Time Big Results is based on the four principles of Purpose, Profit, Productivity and Play. If you want a profitable business in 20 hours a week or less, you need to have...

PURPOSE **be full of purpose, heart and vision**	PROFIT **make great money in tiny pockets of time**
• A clear purpose for your business • A compelling vision of what you want to be known for • A business that plays to your sweet spot of experience, knowledge and expertise • A magnetic big picture • A strong statement that outlines **what** you do and **who** you do it for	• Leveraged products and services where you sell value, not time • Knowledge of your numbers! • Low costs • A strategic and deliberate client attraction strategy • A proven client attraction strategy that works to your strengths in the time you have • A solid and effective client conversion strategy • An aim to create raving fans for life!

PRODUCTIVITY **maximise every minute you have**	PLAY **care for your inner world to create a stunning outer world**
• A decluttered mind • Laser-like focus • Clearly defined working time • Accountability • Delegating for growth • Strong boundaries	• Strong self-belief • Trust in your value • A vibe that matches the frequency of your goals and the people you're here to serve • Time off for rest and recovery • Fun!

CHAPTER 29: YOUR NEXT STEP

Information doesn't create results; implementation does. The aim of this book has been to equip you with the principles and methodology you can use to make your business work in 20 hours a week or less.

NOW IT'S TIME FOR YOU TO TAKE ACTION.

Your first port of call is to join the Tiny Time Book Club, download and complete the workbook. Join here: www.yasminvorajee.com/jointtbookclub/

Your next step is to begin implementing, step by step...

- Define what you do

- Get clear on who you do it for

- Create your signature program and think about different offers based on budget levels and entry points

- Decide how you will market offline and online, and the methods that work to your strengths and for your ideal client

- Focus on how you will generate leads

- Master how you turn prospects into clients (your sales process)

- Delight your clients and turn them into raving fans

- Build leverage into your programs, services, processes and systems so you can grow and scale with ease

You could do this alone, or if you prefer support, with me and a like-minded community. Being a business owner can be a solitary affair. If you find it hard to hold yourself accountable, or start off with great passion and enthusiasm but it wanes quickly and you know you need support and a firm-but-loving approach to grow your business, I recommend joining the Tiny Time Business School.

The Tiny Time Business School combines the concepts covered in this book with a lot more detail on the practicalities. It also provides practical implementation support on a weekly basis.

You can read more about the program here: www.yasminvorajee. com/tinytimebusinessschool

If you are looking for one-on-one support, I provide this to a very limited number of private clients. (I have tiny time after all!) You can get in touch at support@yasminvorajee.com to discuss further.

FINALLY...

Thank you for spending this time with me, I know how precious your tiny time is so it has been a privilege!

Here's to the dream of a purposeful, profitable, productive and playful 20-hour week business! I know you can do this.

It's time to trust yourself and move mountains... one tiny step at a time.

All my best,

Yasmin x

P.S. I would love to hear how you have used the Tiny Time Big Results methodology in your business! You can email me at support@ yasminvorajee.com!

CHAPTER 30: RESOURCES & RECOMMENDED READING

Join the Book Club:
https://www.yasminvorajee.com/jointtbookclub/ and get access to

- The Tiny Time Big Results Workbook

- A monthly live Q&A Call with Yasmin

- 5 Steps to Attract & Convert Clients in 20 Hours A Week – free video series

- Leverage Mastery Cheatsheet: How to Turn One Program into Multiple Streams of Income

- 15 Ways to Market Your Business in Tiny Pockets of Time

- Top 20 Time-Saving, Money Making Tools

- 17 Fool-proof Ways to Turn Your Lukewarm Audience into Eager Buyers

Find out more about the Tiny Time Business School: https://www.yasminvorajee.com/tinytimebusinessschool/

Books That Have Inspired Me

- *Ask And It Is Given* by Esther & Jerry Hicks

- *Leveraging the Universe* by Mike Dooley

- *Wishes Fulfilled* by Wayne Dyer

- *You'll See It When You Believe It* by Wayne Dyer

- *Key Person of Influence* by Daniel Priestley

- *Oversubscribed* by Daniel Priestley

- *Deep Work* by Cal Newport

- *The Gifts of Imperfection* by Brene Brown

- *Supercoach* by Michael Neill

- *The Game of Life* by Florence Scovel Shinn

- *Rise Sister Rise* by Rebecca Campbell

- *Light is The New Black* by Rebecca Campbell

- *Virtual Freedom: How to Work with Virtual Staff* by Chris Ducker

- *The Science of Selling* by David Hoffeld

- *I Hope I Screw This Up* by Kyle Cease

- *Dare to Dream Bigger* by Clare Josa

- *Your Book is The Hook* by Karen Williams

- *The Universe Has Your Back* by Gabrielle Bernstein

- *This Book Means Business* by Alison Jones

- *You Are a Badass* by Jen Sincero

- *You Are A Badass At Making Money* by Jen Sincero

- *Outrageous Openness: Letting the Divine Take the Lead* by Tosha Silver

- *Big Magic* by Elizabeth Gilbert

- *To Sell is Human* by Daniel Pink

- *I, Partridge: We Need to Talk About Alan* By Alan Partridge

PRAISE FOR THE TINY TIME BUSINESS SCHOOL

Making the decision to sign up for Yasmin's Tiny Time Business School was one of the best things I have ever done. It came up at exactly the right time (as these things often do), as I decided to return to my business (laughter yoga) after taking a break for a year due to family commitments. I wanted to make my "comeback" as professional as possible, and be even better than I was before.

I love the fact that all the modules are in bite-size pieces, they can easily be fitted into any schedule when you have very little time, they make so much sense and you just want to go and try out Yasmin's suggestions for yourself!! All the modules are full of tips and they really make you think. You can do everything at your own pace, and the weekly live calls are very helpful. Yasmin is really helpful and approachable, which helps make doing the course an enjoyable process.

I have already implemented some of the suggestions, and they have really made a difference. My marketing is definitely a lot more streamlined, professional looking and targeted to the right people. Opportunities have opened up for me as a result of taking the right action consistently. I would recommend Tiny Time Business School to anybody – you learn so much – you'll be glad you signed up!

Thanks Yasmin!

Karen McGonigle, Laughter Yoga Specialist

I LOVE working with Yasmin, love her Tiny Time Business School program and her coaching! Honestly, I think this is one of our best investments we've made. We have taken over the business recently which needed a lot of improvement and we needed to get our heads around it.

Yasmin's program and especially coaching helped us (and still is helping) to get our heads around our main message and how we want to communicate it with people. I highly recommend working with Yasmin because it gave us clarity.

It felt like Yasmin was the only one with a torch in that dark tunnel and was showing us the way, leading us. There is a lot of information online and I have wasted a lot of my time and energy looking at different things and trying to figure it out myself.

The beauty of Yasmin's program is that you learn the techniques and then she explains how exactly to use it in our own business with our specific product.

Sometimes I just love to ask Yasmin's opinion and get her reassurance – it plays a huge part in our business. When we have doubts, Yasmin always reminds us of our vision and brings back the confidence and belief.

Yasmin helped us to discover and create our core offer, promote it and get paid for it really well. We are very close to recouping the investment back in 2 months (in a 3 month program) but I can see how much more business this program will be bringing to us going forward. Our business was just breaking even before we took over and in the 2 months that we worked with Yasmin, we have started making a profit.

*This is only the start, so I am very excited
to see what future will bring!*

*I would highly recommend Yasmin and her services
to any business owner or entrepreneur.*

Thank you, Yasmin!!

Agne Jonele, Sasta, Carrick on Shannon

*"I invested in the Tiny Time Business School as I already
had got a flavour for Yasmin's style and liked her emphasis
on maximizing the limited time you have available
when you are juggling family and a business.*

*In particular I wanted to get up to speed on designing landing
pages, building my email list and creating compelling opt in gifts.*

My marketing skills also needed to be upgraded.

Tiny Time Business School did not disappoint!

*I love that I can refer back to specific modules
when I need to fill a gap in my knowledge.*

*If you want to become more efficient in your business and make it
work on your limited time then go for Tiny Time Business School"*

Miriam Reilly, Founder of Authentic Love Academy

A TINY TIME BUSINESS MANIFESTO

A 20-hour week business owner...

1. Values her time and sees it as precious and sacred

2. Craves meaningful work and wants to make a difference

3. Works smarter, not harder

4. Focuses on her zone of genius

5. Desires money because it gives her the freedom she dreams of

6. Knows she can be far more productive in fewer hours

7. Doesn't buy into the 24/7 hustle mentality

8. Knows it's what you do with the time you have that counts

9. Hones in on results and outcomes, not time spent.

10. Is willing and open to create a mindset around leverage to make her life simpler.

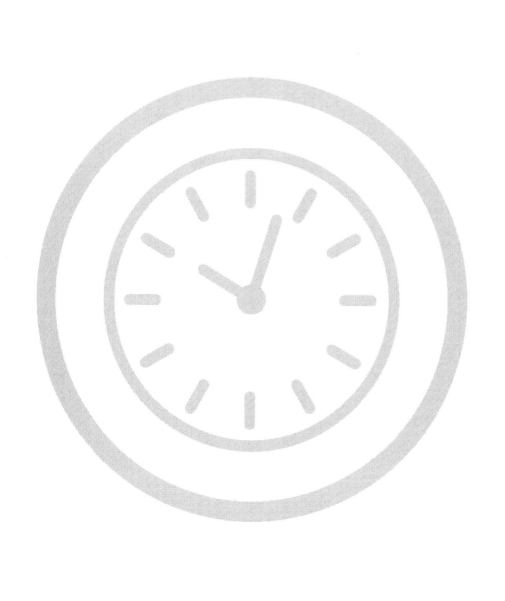

ABOUT YASMIN

Yasmin Vorajee, creator of Tiny Time Big Results, helps small business owners run a profitable business in 20 hours a week or less. A former Vice President of Leadership Development, Yasmin specialises in business and marketing strategy and runs her thriving business from her home in rural Ireland where she lives with her husband and their 3 young children.

Yasmin is from the UK and has lived in Ireland for the last 17 years. She is passionate about helping people create fulfilment in their work and financial abundance so families can spend more time together, connect deeply and enjoy life fully.

Yasmin has featured in the Irish Times, the Irish Independent, Dublin City FM, The Huffington Post, Tatler Magazine, Tesco Magazine, Evoke and the Sunday Independent. She also featured in the Global Women & Leadership Summit along speakers including Cherie Blair and Marianne Williamson.

Yasmin helps small business owners to

- **Nail** your marketing **message** so it's **clear, compelling and magnetic!**

- **Design products and programs** that make it easy for you to be profitable in 20 hours a week (*or less*)

- **Create** and **implement** an **authentic** and **powerful marketing** strategy

- **Manage your energy, not time** and get the right things done (*the things that actually make a difference!*). No more being **glued to your phone** or laptop all the time!

On a personal note, Yasmin loves food and you'll find her either making it, eating it or thinking about it!

Connect with Yasmin

- Join the Tiny Time Book Club: www.yasminvorajee.com/jointtbookclub/
- Join the free Tiny Time Tribe Facebook Group: www.facebook.com/groups/tinytimetribe
- Take 30 seconds and 'Like' Tiny Time Big Results on Facebook: www.facebook.com/tinytimebigresultswithYasminVorajee
- Email Yasmin at support@yasminvorajee.com
- Follow Yasmin on Twitter @tinytimewithyas
- Connect with Yasmin on Linkedin
- Follow Yasmin on Instagram @yasvorajee
- Subscribe to Yasmin's YouTube Channel here http://www.youtube.com/yasminvorajee
- For media, print or podcast interview, please contact support@yasminvorajee.com

ACKNOWLEDGEMENTS

This is where it gets emotional! I have to start off by thanking my parents, Bilkis and Sikander for being the most amazing, kind-hearted and generous souls who walked this planet. I would not be the person I am today without you. You have been by my side every step of the way, even when it was not easy, and every day I am so thankful for your love and support.

To Colm, Fionn Hamza, Zayna Maebh and Daire Idris. Everything I do is for you guys and I love you so much. Thank you for cheering me on and for your patience, even when I got cranky! You are my world and kids, I am so blessed you chose me to be your mum. Colm, thanks for letting me be your current wife! ;)

For Sabiha, my gorgeous sister. You have been with me always and in all ways. Support and love doesn't even begin to describe what you mean to me and how much you have helped me – emotionally, mentally, spiritually and physically. A million thank you's and I love you's will never be enough.

Bilal – my lovely brother. Thank you for tormenting me to play Batman with you when we were kids (*who am I kidding, it was last month!*) and thank you for letting me watch you become a fantastic husband and incredible father to your daughters. It is a joy to witness. Your sense of fun and passion for things that fire you up are a constant inspiration and I love you so much.

For my sweet parents in law, Padraig and Theresa (and Noodles) – thank you for welcoming me into your family and for your love and generosity over the years and for keeping the children stocked up with chocolate rolls!

For my family – who have always been there for me and I am blessed you are in my life. Salma, Khadijah, A'ishah, Zahraa, Dearbhla, Paul, Tara, Roisin, Ronan, Enda, Helen, Grace, Aimee, Cathal, Eve, Aoife, Will (Holly), Ayesha, Fatima (Gorima), Cassim (Gorabjaee), Amine, Nur-ul-Huda, Abdullah, Little Khadijah, Amma, Shirin (Munnie Khala), Yahya (Masajee), Idris, Junaid, Adam, Safiyyah, Zakiyyah, Masud, Majid, Majeeda, Sumeyya, Mehzabin, Shahid, Tammy, Mary Murphy and all my family in the UK, Ireland and India.

For my lovely uncle, Cassim, who passed away this year, you are always in our hearts and prayers. You are so missed.

For my friends – this is the bit where I panic I'm going to miss someone!! Over the years, I have been blessed with incredible friends. Thank you to my friends from my corporate days in Chester and Carrick. Thank you to my Red Tent ladies who keep my cup filled. Thank you to my friends at the school gate. Thank you to the fabulous people of Carrick who make this one of the best places to live in the world. Thank you to my Professional Speaking Association friends who make networking so much fun. For my Facebook friends, you make being online a joy! A big thank you to all my friends - those I see regularly and those I haven't seen in ages, I cherish you all!

For everybody who has helped me get this book out into the world. Starting with my editor, Kris Emery – it was a joy and privilege to work with you. For Antony and Cheryl at eBook Designs, thank you for the gorgeous cover and interior. For the guidance and mentorship of Alison Jones, Karen Williams, Joanna Penn and Clare Josa. For my test readers, Hattie Voelcker, Meg Lyons, Kate Reynolds, Samantha Dunnage and Dara Caryotis, your feedback was invaluable and your input helped me tremendously! Thank you!

An enormous thank you to the Tiny Time Street Team for your support, kindness and focus in spreading the word! You are listed in the next page and you are fantastic!

Finally, a BIG thank you to all my lovely clients and the Tiny Time community, this book is for you.

Yasmin xxx

THE TINY TIME STREET TEAM

Violet Aecor, Rachel Aiken, Linda Anderson, Trudy Arthurs, Uzma Asghar, Michelle Baxter, Gertie Drury O'Beirne, Susan Bourke, Jenny Brennan, Eamonn O'Brien, Karen Brown, Emma Burford, Michelle Carney, Dara Caryotis, Victoria Mary Clarke, Linda Compton, Vanessa Cooney, Eadaoin Curtin, Rani Dabrai, Inga Deksne, Karen O'Donnell, Sinead Dundon, Jackie Elton, Damien Faughnan, Denise Fay, Eric Fitzpatrick, Amanda Jane Fisher, Ruth Fox, Aoife Gaffney, Pamela Galligan, Moira Geary, Nicola Goodhew, Lynsey Hanratty, Lottie Hearn, Sharon Huggard, Agne & EJ Jonele, LaCourdia Jones, Luisa Kearney, Tomi Kareis, Kapil Khanna, Kate Knowler, Fiona Kearns, Sarah Leather, AJ Leggett, Cassi Lowe, Amy Lynch, Mark Lyons, Meg Lyons, James Martin, Niamh McCarthy, Fiona McGuire, Sarah McKenna, Paula McNicholas, Oonagh Monaghan, Jillian Morkan, Barbara Moynihan, Mary Murphy, Anna Murray, Sandra Pilarczyk, Miriam Reilly, Juliet Robinson, Morena Russell, Nicola Semple, Robin Sherrod, Rachel Smith, Paul Ter Wal, Leon Tunney-Ware, Hattie Voelcker, Fiona Whitfield, Catherine Williams, Michael Wright

Thank you all! And a big thank you to everybody who has supported me in any way you can!

Printed in Poland
by Amazon Fulfillment
Poland Sp. z o.o., Wrocław